I Already Know How to Read

I Already Know How to Read

A Child's View of Literacy

Prisca Martens

Heinemann
Portsmouth, NH

Heinemann
A division of Reed Elsevier Inc.
361 Hanover Street
Portsmouth, NH 03801-3912
Offices and agents throughout the world

Acquisitions Editor: Toby Gordon
Copy Editor: Alan Huisman
Production Editor: Renée M. Nicholls
Cover Designer: Jenny Jensen Greenleaf
Manufacturing Coordinator: Louise Richardson

Credits for borrowed material begin on page 107.

Library of Congress Cataloging-in-Publication Data
Martens, Prisca.
    I already know how to read : a child's view of literacy / Prisca
Martens.
        p.   cm.
    Includes bibliographical references (p.   ).
    ISBN 0-435-07226-9
    1. Reading (Preschool)—Case studies.   2. Literacy—Case studies.
    3. Children—Language—Case studies.   I. Title.
LB1140.5.R4M37   1996
372.4—dc20
                                                                    96-9461
                                                                    CIP

Printed in the United States of America on acid-free paper
99   EB   3   4   5

To

my parents, Paul and Marguerite Bretscher,
who instilled in me a love of learning
and continue to love and support me

my children, Matthew and Sarah,
who daily teach me about life and learning
through their enthusiasm, creativity, and ingenuity

my husband, Ray,
who unconditionally loves, supports, and believes in me,
encouraging me to do and be all that I can
and refusing to allow me to settle for anything less

Contents

Foreword

I HOPE YOU GITE BADR
—from a get-well card by Sarah

Dr. Prisca Martens's daughter, Sarah, has been part of my thinking for more than five years. I have celebrated her achievements, the achievements of Matthew, her older brother, and those of her parents. My file of her writings is almost as thick as my grandchildren's files. The Martens and I have had an extended family relationship at the same time as we have established professional ties. The story of Sarah's literacy development has informed my understandings about how children in a literate society come to understand the properties and nature of the English writing system. It has also let me know that there is so much more to learn.

I want to share two insights I have learned from *I Already Know How to Read: A Child's View of Literacy*. First, I want to discuss the power of this case study to expand our understandings about the learning capacity of young children. And second, I want to consider how this work provides parents, teachers, and researchers with "ways of looking" at young children's growing knowledge about literacy. These "ways of looking" become the foundation upon which support and instruction in literacy development are built.

From the Child's Views of Literacy

Recently, I was in Taiwan, where Sarah spent the first few months of her life. I immediately became aware that children in Taiwan are as surrounded and embedded in print as a continuous part of their lives as children are in the United States. Yet teachers, researchers, and parents have taken the literate context in which we live for granted. We still tend to believe that children only learn to read and write when they are sat down and told how to use the features of written language. We still do not give children the credit they deserve for learning all the time. When they are embedded in a world filled with literacy, children attend to that literacy, ask questions about its function and purpose, and come to understand the ways that the features of the written language help them make sense of their world.

Prisca Martens documents these aspects as she tells Sarah's story in rich detail so that others come to understand the important part that learning plays in each child's literacy development. The rich tapestry that Prisca provides about the language development of one child will inform anyone interested in how children learn to read and write.

Sarah is energetic, friendly, and anxious to celebrate the wonders of her world with those with whom she interacts. She shares her hopes, her dreams, and her disappointments in oral form and in writing whenever there is a reason or purpose to do so. She has written me Valentine's Day cards, Mother's Day greetings, thank-you notes, and get-well cards. Now that she lives hundreds of miles away from me, she writes me letters to share her new experiences.

In her most recent letter, she not only lets me know that she and her brother are moving to a new school, but she also tells me the reason:

> Are [our] other school didn't let me make stories. I'm already on my 2nt one [story]. My first one is called <u>Our Advancer</u> [Adventure]. My 2nd on [one] is called <u>Sarah & Brandi</u>. I illustrated *Our Advancer* by crayon. I Illustrated <u>Sarah and Brandi</u> by pants [paints].

Whenever I get any messages from Sarah, I notice immediately her growing sophistication with language. In her letter (only part of it is shown above), she tells me about activities in her and Matthew's lives that she knows I'm interested in. As I look more closely at the features of her language, I wonder when she learned to underline, and I'm interested in her uses of the abbreviations for *second*. Her spelling is more conventional than it used to be, and I am amused that she spelled *crayon* appropriately (maybe because she uses them more) and has invented her use of *paint*. I notice that her spelling of my name is still conventional. Before she was five, she wrote my name UADI, UEADI, EADI, and JADI. About a year later, she wrote DEAR YEADA. Since she has been seven, she has written my name conventionally.

My celebrations of Sarah's writing are due to my understanding that children are learning all the time. When children speak, write, play, and talk, they provide opportunities for us to discover the knowledge they have about their world, and this includes the literacy in their world. These understandings are the building blocks for future learning, and it is such careful research as Prisca Martens presents here that helps us know more about how humans are always learning and developing their literacy at the same time.

Throughout her book, Prisca shows how to observe children's reading and writing in order to know more about what their marks and their responses to books and other written materials tell us. The more we know about what children do and the more we understand how that relates to what children are learning, the more we see. We have often washed away or thrown away children's early writing without gaining an appreciation of the knowledge and insights about written language that this represents. Young children's reading of books has often been unappreciated and mistaken as simple memorization tasks. Prisca documents a three-year in-depth literacy history of the changes that occurred in Sarah's reading and writing, and she explains how these changes became important to Sarah's growing knowledge about reading and writing. Prisca shows the different kinds of writing children do over time, how spelling becomes more conventional, and how punctuation emerges. She demonstrates how the social environment of the learner impacts literacy development and how the other systems of communication, such as art, are embedded in young children's reading and writing. We come to know that children's engagements with reading and writing from the youngest ages represent their meaningful activity in their social world. Prisca provides a language and a framework that parents, teachers, and researchers can use to explore other children's literacy development in similar ways. This is the only book that documents the journey of a child's literacy history from the age of two, and it represents a growing but still small set of studies about young children coming to understand literacy prior to schooling.

From the Adults' Views of Literacy

Some readers may consider that Sarah's story is unique because she comes from a privileged home where writing and reading are important to the lives of all who live there, where art is part of everyday experiences, and where celebrating the learnings of the children in the family are part of the daily routine. This home is indeed unique, but not simply because of its middle class nature. It is unique in the ways that all homes are unique. People write for specific purposes, and the differences depend on family relationships and how far away family members live from each other. The differences depend on how much time parents take to involve their children in their own daily reading and writing activities and how often they pay attention to the daily activities of their children. Homes everywhere are rich in literacy experiences: some family members fill out forms for a range of services; some read the Bible and discuss its interpretations daily; some are concerned with the politics of their community and write letters to editors or read editorials aloud in concerned voices. Parents use recipes, read instructions on medicine containers, and check the directions on packages of laundry detergent. They read to find out how much fat is included in some food and what is considered diet or decaffeinated.

I Already Know How to Read helps us realize that the daily literacy activities that often occur incidentally in the home help children learn about literacy as much as story reading and journal writing do. Every literacy experience is a potential teacher, especially when the adults help children understand how such writing and reading is important to their lives. In this way, kids come to appreciate that these experiences count as reading and writing.

It becomes the role of the teacher to help children recognize the many ways in which they are already literate when they come to school. It is absolutely necessary to build on what children know and to help them recognize that they do know. When children come to believe that what they bring from home is not worthy in school, they discount their literate behaviors and soon begin to believe that they do not or cannot learn to read and write.

As Prisca examines her transactions with Sarah, she shows how her interest in Sarah's reading and writing activities leads to literacy development. Sarah, a bright child interested in the written world in which she lives, probably reads and writes even more than she would have if Prisca had been a less-interested bystander. Here, Prisca documents Sarah's search for answers to her own questions about how literacy worked for her. Further, the interactions between researcher (mother) and informant (daughter) influenced Sarah to expand on her uses of reading and writing and to talk about literacy with an interested adult who took her seriously. Prisca's excitement and interest in Sarah's reading and writing were evident to Sarah, and she responded with an intense focus on literacy as a mode of communication and social interaction.

Such interactions are available to parents, teachers, and researchers. Prisca's work provides the opportunity and the framework for Sarah's hope that we all "gite badr." We need to get better at observing what children do during their reading and writing. We need to get better at appreciating the knowledge that our observations reveal a lot about what children know. We need to get better at conversing with kids while they are engaged in their reading and writing, and we need to take their works seriously and respond with respect. We need to get better at supporting children's literacy development by recognizing what they do as reading and writing that become the building blocks for their lifelong development. And we need to get better at celebrating children's explorations and understanding the power of their learning. This book will help us start.

—Yetta Goodman

Acknowledgments

I used to believe, naively, that authors thought of ideas and worked pretty much alone to put them on paper. The experience of writing this book has taught me otherwise. I now know that without the help and support of numerous other books, this one would not be in existence.

My close and special friends and mentors, Yetta and Ken Goodman at the University of Arizona, have tirelessly supported, encouraged, and believed in me and helped me see things in myself I didn't know were there. They've responded to drafts, offered insights and suggestions, and freely given up writing samples Sarah created for them. They have greatly influenced me as a thinker, researcher, teacher, reader, and writer.

My other mentors at the University of Arizona—Kathy Short, Terri McCarty, and Dana Fox—have also greatly inspired me and impacted my thinking. These mentors all guided me through the initial data collection, analysis, and writing of my dissertation, out of which this book grew. Their friendship and support was, and continues to be, invaluable.

Friends and family members, particularly Terri Tarkoff, Wendy Hood, and my parents, Paul and Marguerite Bretscher, willingly let me confiscate letters, notes, and pictures Sarah created for them so I could have the originals in my data.

Other friends have supported me in a variety of ways. Denny Taylor encouraged me and helped me make initial contacts with Heinemann. Nancy Gahl, Jerry Harste, Sue Mau, Debbie Thomas, and Michael Parsons read portions of drafts; Ann Reiser loaned me her office over Christmas vacation so I could attempt to stay on schedule; Beth Berghoff read drafts and helped with teaching so I could meet deadlines; Chris Leland, Mike Cohen, Barbara Wilcox, Steve Bialostok, Gail Pritchard, Kathleen Crawford, and numerous others listened to me and offered endless encouragement.

My brothers—Joel Bretscher, who helped with graphics; Nathan Bretscher, who pushed me to believe I could accomplish this; Paul

Bretscher; Seth Bretscher; Matthew Bretscher—and my sisters—Bethel Crockett; Sarah Stoehr; Monica Shafer; and Rachel McMillan—along with their families, encouraged and supported me along the way.

My brother-in-law Gary Martens provided long-distance technical and computer assistance at all hours of the day and night. He, along with my other extended family, Eldon Martens, Earl Martens, and Helen Tuttle—and their families—have continually supported me.

The editorial staff at Heinemann, including Toby Gordon, Renée M. Nicholls, Jenny Jensen Greenleaf, Alan Huisman, and Louise Richardson patiently led me through the publishing process.

My family unselfishly accepted my absences during the long hours of writing. My husband, Ray, cooked, cleaned, washed, and shopped, and my children, Matthew and Sarah, worked, played, and patiently waited for me to return, always with open arms and loving hearts that welcomed me.

To all of these I extend my gratitude and thanks for helping me experience and learn about writing and publishing this book.

1

Learning to See

On a crisp February morning, Sarah and her visiting Aunt Elaine were chatting in the back seat of the family van. They were talking about Sarah's upcoming fifth birthday, in June, and how she would enter kindergarten in the fall, something Sarah was eagerly anticipating. Aunt Elaine asked, "What are you going to do in kindergarten? Are you going to learn how to read?" Without hesitation Sarah replied emphatically, "I already know how to read!"

Coming from a child whose reading some would refer to as "memorization" and whose writing was not readable to anyone unfamiliar with it, "I already know how to read!" might be dismissed as wishful thinking, true only in her imagination. From her perspective, however, Sarah *was* literate: every day she used reading and writing to make sense of and organize her life in natural and authentic ways and to situate herself as a unique participant in her family and social community.

And if asked, Sarah could substantiate her claim by producing examples:

- Wanting to go to her friend Krystal's house to play, Sarah drew a map to remind her father how to get from her door to Krystal's door without getting lost. She had seen him draw maps to help people find our house and knew he pointed out landmarks. Sarah, recently turned four, incorporated "landmarks" important to her in her map.

- Sarah's fourth birthday—the fun, the excitement, her party, the gifts—lingered in her mind long after she blew out the candles. She began planning for her fifth birthday when it was still more than nine months away, writing lists, anytime, anywhere, almost daily for a while, of friends she wanted to remember to invite to her party.
- Sarah loved books. Her father and I read to her daily, and she regularly picked up her favorite books and read them to herself and others, integrating her knowledge of the plot, cues in the illustrations, and the story language she remembered.
- As a toddler, Sarah proudly read environmental print in her home and community—cereal boxes, labels, stop signs, K-Mart and Target signs, signs for the local grocery stores Frys and Safeway, McDonald's and Walt Disney logos.
- Sarah used her knowledge of story from her experiences with books to write her own stories. Sometimes she wrote them with pencil or crayon on paper; other times she typed them on the computer, as she saw her father and me do, patiently and determinedly finding each letter she wanted.
- For Valentine's Day, Sarah designed her own valentine cards for her family and friends.

Sarah knew what reading and writing were because she saw them being used in her world. She read for a variety of personal and social purposes: to gain information, for personal enjoyment, for survival, to participate in routines and activities with others, and so on. And she wrote for a variety of personal and social purposes: to enrich social relationships, to help her remember, to entice and persuade, to participate in the community, and so on. No setting was unconducive for literacy: she read and wrote at home, in church, at the doctor's office, in the car while running errands, everywhere. The literacy interwoven into her social community shaped who she was as a reader and a writer (Taylor 1983). Reading and writing breathed life into her existence just as air did. Both were natural and necessary. Based on these kinds of documented literacy events, Sarah stated she already knew how to read and write.

Seeing What We Know

Jean Piaget believed that we don't "know what we see"; we "see what we know" (Piaget 1971). He understood that our belief systems are the lens through which we interpret the world. What we believe about children and how they learn determines what and how we interpret their statements and actions. We cannot "see" outside our frame of reference.

For most of my seventeen years of teaching, I did not "see" as I do now. Because of my beliefs about children, learning, and literacy, I would have listened to Sarah's "I already know how to read!" and dismissed the statement as untrue. I saw and believed reading to be decoding words accurately and writing to be forming letters and spelling correctly. Children couldn't decode words or spell until they knew the letters of the alphabet and their sounds. I saw the "reading" children did of books and environmental print as precursors to reading, but certainly not "real" reading. I saw the marks and scribbles children made on paper as precursors to writing, but certainly not "real" writing.

Therefore, to lay the necessary foundation and move my kindergarten students to "real" reading and "real" writing, I organized my classroom around studying a new letter of the alphabet each week. For homework the children found pictures of items beginning with the sound associated with the letter we were studying. Eventually the children put the pictures together into an alphabet book. When we knew enough letters and sounds to make a word, we studied the word and practiced decoding it. When we knew enough words to write a sentence, we wrote the sentence and practiced reading it. The children read from ability-ranked readers so that they could successfully decode the words. We wrote class stories about events and experiences and circled the words we knew. We practiced writing the letters and words, forming the letters correctly, and staying on the lines of the paper.

What I "saw" in all this classroom activity was how well the children performed what I designed for them to do. My best students were the ones who could write or circle the letter representing the beginning sound of a picture on a worksheet, form letters neatly and correctly on the lines of the paper, and accurately read the stories in the graded readers. They were successful, I believed, because of their knowledge and the wealth of rich literacy experiences they had had. My poor students were the ones who could not identify which letter represented the beginning sound of a picture, formed letters incorrectly, couldn't stay on the lines even if they tried (which I never believed they really did), couldn't decode words or read the graded readers, and couldn't remember a word from one line to the next even when I prompted them. They were unsuccessful, I believed, because of their lack of knowledge and effort and a paucity of literacy experiences.

Then what I knew began to change. I participated in the National Writing Project at Arizona State University (ASU), became interested in what I heard and learned, and enrolled in graduate courses in reading and writing at ASU and eventually at the University of Arizona. I read articles and books. I joined book groups and discussed literacy issues with other teachers. I became more and more intrigued with the notion that children enter school as experienced language and literacy users, that their knowledge begins at birth and continues to grow throughout their lives, and that they gain this knowledge through natural, functional, authentic experiences with literacy in their everyday social environment. I began to wonder whether my kindergarten students knew more than I was giving them credit for, especially my "poor" students, because I hadn't been interested and hadn't provided opportunities for them to show me what they knew about reading and writing, hadn't known how to "see" that. I realized that perhaps I only saw what I knew and valued (i.e., how conventional, accurate, and correct the products of their reading and writing were) and not all that *the children* knew about literacy.

During my last three years of teaching kindergarten, because my beliefs were changing, I began to see with new eyes. Instead of assuming my students didn't know anything and I needed to teach them everything, I decided to restructure my classroom so I could examine their reading and writing in school more closely and let them teach me what they knew. This was a slow and difficult change for me. I still worried about their knowing letters and sounds so I kept the letter of the week, but dealt with it in a less formal and rigid way. Instead of only decoding words and sentences, we also read big books, predictable books, poems, and the class stories we wrote. Instead of only writing letters of the alphabet and words, accurately and on the lines, we wrote journals, a class newspaper, learning logs, and literature response logs, all on unlined paper. I scheduled a "free reading" time in which students could read with each other and with me. I set up a writing center in which students could make books, cards, letters, or whatever they chose.

Gradually, as I drew on the new knowledge I was learning in my courses and from my reading and let the children teach me what *they* knew, I began "seeing" in a more knowledgeable and informed way. Whereas once I too had dismissed their reading of familiar stories and pattern books as "memorization" I now saw them following the print, using picture cues, knowing when to turn the page, self-correcting themselves if their language didn't fit the language of the story. Whereas once I had viewed their writing as random marks made with no thought, I now saw they were orchestrating their knowledge of what written language looks like and sounds like and their intended meaning to write coherently. I saw them writing, not haphazardly, but from left to right and from the top to the bottom of the page, and experimenting with different fonts, spacing, and punctuation. I began to value the knowledge they had and used to read and write.

My classroom and my teaching were energized. I was excited about going to school every morning. I anticipated what and how the children would read and write that day. I looked for the knowledge about literacy they brought with them every day. What I didn't realize at the time, though, was that while I was seeing more, what I saw was still influenced—and limited—by my beliefs. Yes, I was seeing and appreciating the knowledge the children had. But because I was still concerned with how well their reading and writing resembled accurate and conventional reading and writing, I still focused on, emphasized, and evaluated letter, sound, and word accuracy as "superior" knowledge in the classroom. I valued and regarded highly correct products without appreciating, understanding, and marveling at the literacy process at work in creating those products. And, although I examined and celebrated the literacy the children demonstrated in school, I didn't seriously consider the reading and writing they did at home, how they learned what they knew about reading and writing at home, or what it was about the home environment that stimulated, facilitated, and nurtured this learning.

Seeing and Learning with Sarah

It was then that Sarah became my primary and most influential informant. I began collecting data on her reading and writing when she was two and a half years old (Martens 1994) My son Matthew was five years old at the time and entering kindergarten, and although I had saved some writing he had done through the years, much of his literacy learning had slipped by me unnoticed. I had missed a golden opportunity to observe and study how children gain knowledge about literacy and how literacy is learned in natural settings.

So, unbeknownst to her, I enlisted Sarah as my teacher in some "home schooling." I interacted with her as a mother and child do but was conscious of not purposefully directly teaching her anything. I wanted to understand what and how she learned about literacy through natural everyday events. She had easy access to books, magazines, newspapers, pencils, paper, crayons, and so on, and initiated many literacy events herself. Occasionally I asked whether she wanted me to read to her (she often came and asked me on her own) or suggested that a thank-you note, get-well card, birthday card, or other greeting needed to be written to a friend or relative. Otherwise, if I saw her pick up a book and read, I'd listen and observe from a distance or wander over and ask her to read to me. I spent many hours reading to her and listening to her read to me. We discussed stories, what we liked, why certain incidents were funny, and how the story and pictures were organized. If I found her drawing or writing, I'd observe her for awhile, then ask her what she was doing and whether she'd read me what she'd written. We talked about her writing, where her ideas came from, and how she decided what to write. I asked lots of questions, listened, and tried to get inside her head and see and understand literacy and the literacy process as she did. I watched with intense interest how she selected certain aspects of print, both in books and in her own writing, on which to focus her attention. I was in awe of the sophistication of her thinking and the knowledge and insight she gained and used, all without being directly taught and without studying a letter of the alphabet a week.

Teach me, Sarah did. She forced me to revalue literacy, what it means to read and write, what it means to be a reader and a writer, what it means to be a literate member of a literate society. She forced me to reexamine the conventional "school" notions of learning to read and write that I had lived with, advocated, and taught by for years. She forced me to see what I hadn't seen before, to define literacy and literacy learning in new ways.

As time went on I began to realize that if Sarah had been a student in my kindergarten classroom, I would have seen her as one of my best students. She would have done well circling letters and writing on the lines and she would have decoded the words and sentences in the graded readers fairly easily. But I would not have known her as a literate human being. I would not have known she drew maps, wrote lists, loved to read in the car, and created valentines, all without studying a letter/sound a week. I would not have known what she knew about literacy and would not have seen her as the experienced reader and writer she was. That was a frightening realization. I wondered about all the other "Sarahs" I'd taught and never gotten to know. Even more frightening was wondering what Sarah's kindergarten experience would be like. What if she had a teacher like me, who never asked and didn't value who the children were as literate human beings, who didn't let them teach him or her what they knew about literacy before they ever came to school? What if her kindergarten teacher required the children to study a letter of the alphabet a week and didn't provide opportunities for Sarah and the other children to teach him or her what they knew? What then?

All children's experiences in life and with literacy are different, their personalities are different, the aspects of literacy they attend to at specific times are different, their inventions of reading and writing are different, and the ways in which they refine their inventions are different. While what follows is Sarah's story, it is important, just as all children's stories are important. By looking closely at one child's literacy we learn how to see and how to look and understand other children's literacy. It is my hope that as Sarah taught me to see, her story will enlighten others and help them to see also.

Sarah, like all of us, poses questions for herself about anomalies or perplexities she perceives in her world that she wants to understand. She solves those inquiries by investigating them. The next three chapters of this book is organized around what I perceive are the inquiries over which Sarah puzzles:

- "What are *you* doing with that written language?" Chapter 2 looks at Sarah's investigation of the function and purpose of written language within the community in which she lives.
- "How can *I* read and write?" Chapter 3 examines Sarah's inventions of written language and how they allow her to participate and make meaning as a reader and writer herself in her community.
- "How do *we* read and write?" Chapter 4 explores how Sarah works toward understanding how to communicate in a comprehensible and understandable way with others in her community.

I don't believe these inquiries are conscious. I identified them based on patterns I observed in Sarah's interests, perceptions, behaviors, and inventions. I also don't believe these inquiries are in any way sequenced but occur simultaneously. The constraints of writing about them, however, necessitate doing so one at a time.

2

"What Are You Doing with That Written Language?"

Written language is all around us. It is integral to our lives, so integral that we often don't even realize we're reading and writing. I didn't anyway. Sarah changed that. She heightened my awareness of the reading and writing I do and of how pivotal reading and writing are to my life and to the lives of others. Through her I came to appreciate how critical everyday literacy events are to young children's literacy learning. She drove me to investigate and deepen my own understanding of literacy and what we *do* with written language.

A Literate Environment Nurtures Learning

Sarah was born in Taipei, Taiwan. When she was six months old, she traveled to the United States to be adopted into our family. Her brother Matthew, born in Calcutta, India, was three years old at the time; her father Ray was a professional artist who worked in his studio at home; I was a kindergarten teacher and graduate student.

From the time Sarah was born she was surrounded by written language. It's unavoidable. We use written language to label cans, milk cartons, and baby food at home; to identify streets, stores, and billboards in the community; and to report news and advertise products and sales in newspapers, magazines, and on TV. Sarah didn't merely live in a garden of print, however. She witnessed members of her family and others transacting with those texts, using reading and writing naturally every day to bring order to and make meaning in their lives. And she participated in literacy events herself. As an infant she observed her father read the newspaper, art magazines, coupons, and recipes; draw and paint landscapes and figures; and write notes and lists. She saw me read books, calendars, schedules, and catalogs; write lesson plans and memos; and type letters and research papers on the computer. She sat on my lap and listened as I read stories to her and Matthew. As she grew older she held and turned the pages of the books, helped cut out coupons from the newspaper, and suggested items for the grocery list. In each of these literacy events, the written language was often presented in conjunction with other ways of representing and communicating meaning: math symbols, art, music, and so on. (At the time I didn't realize the significance of that, but Sarah did.)

Matthew was and continues to be a special and unique catalyst to Sarah's growing understanding of literacy—as she was and is to his. As her sibling-peer, Matthew demonstrates that *everyone*, not only adults, reads, writes, and uses written language for specific purposes. When Sarah was young she observed Matthew draw pictures, write stories, and read books, signs, logos, and his own writing. As she grew older and was physically able to manipulate books and crayons herself, she participated with Matthew in reading, drawing, playing, and writing, events and activities they continue to do together. They were, and are, models and resources for each other, catalysts stimulating and facilitating each other's learning, actively and reactively shaping literacy experiences for each other (Taylor 1983).

Sarah observed and participated in literacy events in the community as well as at home. She watched members of the congregation sing hymns from hymnals and read the Bible and Sunday school lessons at church. She observed salespeople in bookstores read titles, discuss literature, and write out receipts. She witnessed me and other shoppers read labels and coupons and check off grocery lists at the supermarket, and helped me locate the items on our list (breakfast cereals were a favorite).

I cannot directly observe Sarah's "What are *you* doing with that written language?" investigation. It's "invisible." Whenever Sarah reads "Target" or "McDonald's," picks up a favorite book and reads it, or writes lists or messages to accompany her drawings, she demonstrates that she understands what we "do" with written language: we communicate meaning for specific functions and purposes in our social world. The meaning she creates in each instance documents that understanding.

How did she learn this? It happened naturally as she witnessed and experienced functional, meaningful transactions between written language, others, and herself (Goodman & Altwerger 1980; Hall 1985; Harste, Woodward, & Burke 1984; Leichter 1984; Taylor 1983; Taylor & Dorsey-Gaines 1988; and others).

Forms and Aspects of Written Language

In exploring what we "do" with written language, children must sort through and deal with a number of complexities that are so second nature to us as literate adults that we forget that only as children come to grips with them do they enhance and sharpen their understanding of written language.

Distinguishing Between Drawing and Writing

Initially children do not distinguish between drawing and writing. Writing to them is a form of drawing (Ferreiro & Teberosky 1982), both serving the same function and purpose. It is as they participate in rich functional literacy events that children discover they can represent names and properties of objects in writing that they are unable to represent in their drawings (Ferreiro

1991). They learn that while lines and shapes are used in both, the lines and shapes are organized in different and distinct ways, depending on whether they are representing meaning in writing or in drawing (Ferreiro 1990).

Sarah had countless opportunities to observe drawing, reading, and writing used for a variety of purposes by members of her family and others in the community. She studied the illustrations and written texts in stories and other print, and she manipulated pencils and books herself. These experiences laid the foundation for her to be able to make the drawing/writing distinction.

Sarah began making this distinction when she was two and a half years old. She would draw circular forms separately from and in contrast to a number of horizontal parallel lines (see Figure 2-1)[1], sometimes referring to these lines as writing and reading them to me. Or she would take a text someone else had written and draw circular forms above or below that text. Her circular art forms contrasting with the linear lines of written text reflect the organization of text and illustrations found in picture books and on signs and labels, revealing her understanding that written language exists and serves a function and purpose different from drawing.

Environmental Print

Environmental print labels, names, directs, and identifies. Found on t-shirts, buses, coupons, cars, license plates, posters, the telephone, the computer, and toys, it provides Sarah with inescapable encounters with written language in a social context. The meaning and purpose of environmental print are directly related to its immediate physical setting: it says what it says because of where it is located (the front of a cereal box, the name on a store, highway directional signs). People act or react in specific ways after reading environmental print. Through her observation and participation in literacy events involving environmental print, Sarah learned that written language communicates meaning and is used and necessary for specific purposes (Hall 1987).

---

1. Throughout this book, wherever the translation of Sarah's writing is not explicit, I provide the translated meaning under the letters. If she has handwritten the sample, I often first clarify and reorient her letters based on my experience with her writing techniques and on what she has told me she means.

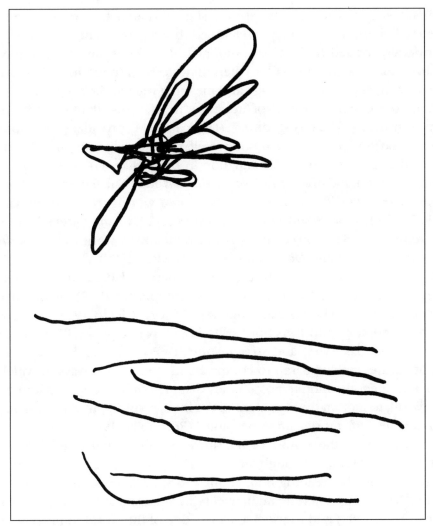

Figure 2-1. Sarah distinguishes between drawing and writing.

Children's Literature (Connected Discourse)

Children's literature played a significant role in deepening Sarah's understanding of what we do with written language. While environmental print is related to its physical setting, children's literature (as well as other forms of connected discourse) is not. Through the stories she gravitated to, poured over, and begged to hear over and over Sarah learned that regardless of where the books are physically located (in her bedroom, Matthew's bedroom, the living room, church, or the car) and no matter when they are read (bedtime, mid-morning, or after lunch) the story's language and meaning remain the same.

The "transforming power" of literature "to take you out of yourself and return you to yourself—a changed self" (Huck 1990, 4) provided Sarah with numerous opportunities to learn about herself, life, language, and the world. She stimulated and stretched her imagination in books like *Who's Peeking at Me?* (Moerbeek 1988) and *The Little Mouse, the Red Ripe Strawberry, and the Big Hungry Bear* (Wood & Wood 1984). She visited worlds she never dreamt existed in books like *Bright and Beautiful* (Stowell 1976) and *Snowy Day* (Keats 1962; remember, Sarah lived in Tucson, Arizona!). In stories like *Goodnight Moon* (Brown 1947) and *More More More* (Williams 1990) she came to understand her own and other cultures. She learned and delighted in language through books like *Chicka Chicka Boom Boom* (Martin 1989) and learned social concepts through books like *Sometimes I Share* (Ziefert 1991). She considered the impossible and the choices life holds in books like *Where the Wild Things Are* (Sendak 1963) and *Strega Nona* (DePaola 1975). Even as a young child, literature enabled Sarah to comprehend "the myriad ways in which human beings meet the infinite possibilities that life offers . . . to reap knowledge of the world, to fathom the resources of the human spirit, [and] to gain insights that [made her] life more comprehensible" (Rosenblatt 1983, 6–7).

Captivated by the power of literature, Sarah gained other knowledge about life and literacy through her experiences with it. She developed a "global sense of what reading is all about and what it feels like" (Bissex 1980, 130). She learned to differentiate between the linguistic message and the illustrations (Wells 1985) and to use her knowledge of the world to make sense of and respond to text. She learned that the written language of stories and the spoken language of everyday life are not identical, that there are phrases we read that are not part of typical speech ("once upon a time" or "she replied") and phrases we speak that we usually do not read ("um" or "yeah, right!") (K. Goodman 1994). She learned how to "talk like a book" (Hall 1987, 35) and how stories are structured. She learned that different authors have different writing styles and that literature comes in a variety of genres, among them fairy tales, realistic fiction, and poetry. She learned that readers hold a book, read the print, and use words such as *page* and *front* when referring to the book. Above all, her desire and motivation to read were ignited and fueled through literature. She developed a positive attitude and realized that reading is worth the effort and that literature is highly valued in our culture.

Physical Characteristics

Written language is everywhere, but learning about it is not as simple and straightforward a task for a young child as it may seem. The print around us may all be written language, but that written language does not all look the same. Its physical characteristics can be quite varied. The print identifying "McDonald's" differs from the print identifying "Toys Я Us," which differs from the print identifying the toothpaste as "Crest," which differs from the print identifying a soft drink as "Coca Cola," which differs from the print in the newspaper, which differs from the print in books. There is even a variation in print from book to book and from page to page. The shapes, sizes, case (upper or lower), fonts, and colors of print all vary, sometimes greatly. Not only that, the handwriting of different people—Ray, Matthew, Sarah, me—also varies. Children face an enormous task in sorting through, understanding, and using written language.

Sarah, like all children, had to learn that while the examples of written language she sees take many forms, there are only twenty-six letters. The same letters can be represented in different sizes, shapes, colors, and fonts. She must learn which different forms to treat as the same to get to the meaning. At the same time, she is learning that size, shape, color, and font can be used to enhance meaning. Children learn to handle such ambiguity not by being given single tasks on a worksheet, but by experiencing written language in all its complexity in natural, purposeful everyday use. It's all around them, and they make sense of it as they use it to meet their own needs in their community. The marvel of our brains is that it sorts through the ambiguities of our language with amazing ease (K. Goodman 1993).

Socialization Nurtures Literacy

Literacy is intrinsic to Sarah's experiences. It is woven into the fabric of her life as a tool for making social connections with others, expressing herself, and exploring the world alone or with others (Dyson 1989). As she observes written language being used and uses it herself in meaningful ways to achieve particular goals, she not only knows what literacy looks like but also recognizes its importance, what it means and how and why it is used (Szwed 1988). Frank Smith, in *Joining the Literacy Club* (1988), states that young children learn to be literate—"usually without anyone being aware that they are learning—by participating in literate activities with people who know how and why to do these things. They join the literacy club" (9).

While no other child's experiences with literacy are identical to Sarah's, all children in our society experience reading and writing in their world. The amount of print and the degree of interaction with print vary. Some children, like Sarah, spend thousands of hours being read to, writing, drawing, running errands with family members—all with varying emphases for a variety of functions and purposes—before they enter school. Other children's experiences are more limited. These are the experiences that ignite and fuel the inquiry "What are *you* doing with that written language?"

Sarah's inquiry into "What are *you* doing with that written language?" will never be totally answered. It continues to take on new forms and emphases that will tickle her curiosity and propel her literacy throughout her life. All of us continually discover aspects and functions of written language of which we were previously unaware or didn't need. As Sarah grew and gained experience, she discovered birthday party invitations, eye charts, restaurant menus, word puzzles, video games, journals, dictionaries, and telephone directories. While the specific form of written language varies with the purpose, written language's function of communicating meaning remains the same.

3

"How Can I Read and Write?"

December 1990. Ray, Matthew, Sarah, and I have been driving for two long days from Tucson, Arizona, to northern Montana to spend Christmas with Ray's parents. We arrive at dusk on a cold, dreary afternoon. We scramble from our car into the house to stretch and visit briefly before tackling unloading. Matthew and Sarah go off exploring while Ray, his parents, and I settle in the living room. We have been chatting for no more than ten minutes when Sarah, two and a half, races up to me, waving a small scrap of paper in one hand and clutching a pencil in the other, and excitedly instructs, "Read this! Read this!" I take the paper from her and see she has used the pencil to make several horizontal wavy lines. I suggest that rather than me read it to her, she read it to me. She replies, "I can't."

Even though Sarah didn't read her lines to me, this was a landmark event. It was the first time she demonstrated her understanding that if she, all by herself, made marks on paper, those marks would be laden with meaning that others could read. Her "roots of literacy" (Y. Goodman 1980), which had been digging deeper and deeper into the soil of her literate environment, were now sprouting in her writing. As she was understanding *that* written language makes sense, she was also exploring and inventing for herself *how* it makes sense (Y. Goodman 1984).

Up until that December day I never would have entertained seriously the possibility that Sarah's marks were writing or her responses to signs and books were reading. Her wavy lines certainly weren't even close to being conventional representations of writing. I would have thought they were "cute" and "precursors" to literacy but certainly not evidence of literacy as I know and use it in our literate society.

Sarah made me see, understand, and appreciate the literacy learning process in a new way, from a different perspective. Through the window her reading and writing opened, she taught me that even though her and my reading and writing don't "look" the same, we share a common continuous process of literacy learning, a process that begins at birth and never ends. What makes our literacy products appear different on the surface *isn't* a difference in the process but in how proficiently we control the process; and proficiency and control of the process are directly related to how much experience or "practice" we have had with literacy (Y. Goodman 1992; Harste et al. 1984).

How is Sarah gaining control of the literacy process? How is she getting the experience she needs to read and write more proficiently? What she does *not* do is patiently sit back and wait to be taught. Having identified reading and writing as distinct, important activities she can be proud of accomplishing (Hall 1987), she actively and aggressively reads and writes. Even as a toddler she responded to signs and logos in her environment and selected favorite books to read, sometimes to others and other times out loud to no one in particular. She grasped a pencil, intentionally made marks or wavy lines on paper, and read them herself or expected others to bring meaning to and read them. Her created symbols on paper represent meaning, and through those symbols she constructs meaning socially with others (Dyson 1989).

As a young child Sarah invented, and even now continues to invent, literacy by hypothesizing and predicting how she thinks it works (K. Goodman 1993). She reads and writes by using all the knowledge she has gathered from her experiences up to a particular point in time to construct meaning through written language, just as all proficient readers and writers do. By presenting and testing her inventions, reflecting on others' understanding and comprehension of them—or their lack thereof—and inventing again, she gains insight into how the literacy process works and learns to control it more proficiently.

Inventing is not new to Sarah or to any child. Infants learn to communicate orally by inventing sounds to meet their social needs—requesting a cookie, pointing out an airplane flying overhead, calling attention to where they've been injured. The adults around them may have difficulty understanding initially but through countless authentic functional transactions with others and others' responses to them, children shape and reshape their oral language inventions until these inventions fit within the boundaries of communication in their social community. Our inventions do not end there. Even as adults, we continue to invent such things as pet names, personal signatures, ideas, spellings, and code words. When we get new ideas, we invent language terms to express the new meanings, such as terms we've created in response to computers.

Sarah's inventions represent her hypotheses, her theories of the world, her worldview, and "make sense to [her] inasmuch as the world ever makes sense to anyone" (Halliday 1980, 16). They are as powerful for her when she first creates them as they were the first time they were invented in the history of the world (Duckworth 1987). They are unique, creative, and ingenious, not unlike the inventions of other children such as Paul (Bissex 1980), Adam (Schickedanz 1990), and Giti (Baghban 1984). By practicing reading and writing and by experimenting with her inventions she gradually, over time, learns to control the process more proficiently, and this control becomes more and more visible in her literacy products. Her process does not change; her proficiency at orchestrating it does.

Sarah Invents How to Read Environmental Print

It's inevitable and unavoidable that Sarah encounters the print in her environment and observes others transacting with it. It's just as inevitable and unavoidable that in her quest to participate fully as a member of the family, community, and culture she has been welcomed and accepted into, that she invents how to read and transact with environmental print. For example:

- By age two and a half Sarah read signs such as McDonald's, Target, and Stop when they appeared in their appropriate contexts.

- On our way home from our Christmas in Montana we stopped to eat at a restaurant in Utah. Our booth was next to a window. Sarah, two years seven months, looked out the window, pointed, and excitedly exclaimed, "Look, Mommy! There's K-Mart!" It wasn't K-Mart but a motel with a large red-and-white sign identifying the K Motel.
- At the grocery store we were shopping for decorations for Sarah's third-birthday cake. While she sat in the cart, she insisted on holding the candied letters that spelled Happy Birthday. As we left the baking aisle, she glided her finger under Happy Birthday and proudly read, "Sarah Martens."
- Sarah, three years one month, noticed an ad in the newspaper for Disney videos. The Disney logo, with the castle and Walt Disney name, was prominently displayed at the bottom of the ad. Sarah, whose favorite video at the time, *Peter Pan*, began with the logo, pointed to Walt Disney and said, "That says *Peter Pan*."
- As we were driving down the street one afternoon in Tucson, Sarah, three years one month, excitedly exclaimed, "Mommy, there's Toys Я Us!" She was pointing to a car dealer's sign that read Cars of Tucson in letters similar in shape, size, colors, and positioning to those on the Toys Я Us sign.
- I was getting hamburger buns out of the package for dinner and Sarah, three years four months, said, "I know where those came from—Frys," pointing to the name Frys (a local grocery store chain) on the package.

Many of Sarah's meanings were not conventional but neither were they random, capricious, or unreasonable. They demonstrated her understanding that print says something and she expects that something to make sense to *her* personally, not only to others. She used the knowledge and understanding she had gained through her experiences with print in relation to herself and others to invent and create meaning for print in specific contexts (Y. Goodman 1983). She created her inventions by negotiating the symbolic meanings, the print contexts, her experience, and the social contexts (Dyson 1989) to make logical predictions of appropriate meanings based on her own knowledge, experience, and understanding. In that, her reading process does not differ from mine or the process of other more experienced readers.

Sarah Invents How to Read Children's Literature

Through children's literature—being read to and interacting with books herself—Sarah learned the power literature has when a reader breathes life into the printed text (Rosenblatt 1978). No book, familiar or new, was intimadating to her. She poured over them all with intense interest and curiosity, reading enthusiastically to herself as well as listening intently when others read to her. She was captivated by the power and appeal of literature that comes from a reader's transaction with the text. Louise Rosenblatt states, "The text is a necessary condition, but is not a sufficient condition, for the re-creation of a particular work. The text is merely an object of paper and ink until some reader responds to the marks on the page as verbal symbols" (1978, 23).

Sarah used her knowledge of story structure and patterns of written language to invent how to read, creating a version of the story that made sense to her, always letting constructing a meaningful text drive her reading (Doake 1985). To read, she integrated a semantic use of the illustrations, her experience with the text, and her knowledge of the language in books to construct a "holistic remembering" of her favorite stories (Matlin 1984). In doing so, she "talked" like a reader of books, not like a reader of signs or labels, revealing her understanding and expectation that books "sound" different from the reading of environmental print.

At one time I regarded Sarah's holistically remembered readings (as well as similar readings by my kindergartners) as her imitations of books or memorized renditions of particular stories. She wasn't really reading, I thought, because she wasn't "reading the words." Then I began to see that my thinking misrepresented and devalued a critical, intrinsically motivated learning strategy that allowed her to control, access, and practice the reading process (Doake 1988). When I examined her readings, I became acutely aware of how she was processing text and building and synthesizing meaning (Mikkelsen 1985), not merely reciting the story.

Experienced readers take cues from the three language systems to construct meaning: the *graphophonic system*, or the relationships between the phonological symbols of oral language and the orthographic symbols of written language; the *syntactic system*, or the grammar or structure of language; and the *semantic-pragmatic system*, or the social and personal meaning language represents in a sociocultural context (K. Goodman 1994). Sarah's reading inventions used two of the three language systems: her knowledge of grammar (the syntactic system) and her knowledge of meaning (the semantic-pragmatic system). The graphophonic system, which relates oral and written language, was less prominent but nevertheless visible to her in the language and written text, providing cues.

Experienced readers integrate their knowledge of these three language systems with general cognitive strategies. When readers begin reading, they *sample* the available information in the text for cues that are productive and useful, *infer* information not supplied in the text, and *predict* or anticipate the information they think is coming. Because inferences and predictions involve taking risks, they are tentative. Readers monitor their meaning making, *confirming* or *disconfirming* their inferences and predictions as they gather new information and *correcting* them if necessary to make sense of the text (K. Goodman 1994).

To illustrate how Sarah used the reading process in the same way as more experienced readers do, let's look at a couple of examples from Sarah's reading of one of her favorite books when she was three years old, *The Mixed-Up Chameleon*, by Eric Carle (1975). Transcripts cannot communicate her enthusiasm, confidence, and intonation, but they do communicate how meaning dominated her reading (Doake 1985). They are a window to how she actively engages and transacts with the text, using cognitive reading strategies and her knowledge of how language works to construct meaning as she reads.

The Mixed-Up Chameleon is the story of a chameleon who is quite satisfied with its life until it sees other animals at the zoo. The chameleon then begins wishing it had particular characteristics of some of those animals. Its wishes come true but it becomes very confused and mixed-up about who it is. When the chameleon gets hungry and is unable to catch a fly as it previously could, it wishes itself back to being a chameleon.

The published text on one page reads, "I wish I could see things far away like a giraffe." Sarah, three years five months, read, "And then the chameleon said, 'I wish I could be tall like . . . see things far away like a giraffe.'" Sarah inferred this page would follow the language pattern on several of the previous pages: "I wish I could be [adjective] like a [noun: animal]." She used her knowledge of language and meaning to predict, "I wish I could be tall like a giraffe." While her prediction would have fit the meaning of the story, she realized it did not match the language of the text as she remembered it, disconfirmed her prediction, and reread.

A similar example occurs toward the end of the story. Here the published text reads:

"I wish I could be like people." Just then a fly flew by.

Sarah read:

And then the chameleon said, "I wish I could be people." . . . And then this spider flew by.

Sarah again inferred, predicted, and constructed meaning, based on her knowledge and experience with language, the world, and the text. She knew a small creature flew by the chameleon and predicted *spider*, probably because she lived in Arizona and was more familiar with spiders than flies. Also, *spider* and *fly* are both nouns, so the syntactic structure of the sentence is maintained. *Spider* made sense to her and she continued without correcting, not significantly disrupting the meaning of the story. Later, when the text read, "And it couldn't catch the fly," she predicted something like, "And he didn't know how to catch the fly," this time reading *fly*. But, again she realized that this prediction, while it is similar and would have been meaningful, didn't fit the language of the text as she remembered it, disconfirmed, and self-corrected.

Sarah's reading of *The Mixed-Up Chameleon* also highlights how she positioned herself in stances other than "recreational reader" in relation to the text. For example, in one place she took the stance of a critic. She pointed to the illustration and commented, "Mommy, the turtle shouldn't be there, the flamingo should be there. . . . The turtle should be right here," testing and comparing her own ideas and opinions on how to arrange the illustrations with the decisions made by the author and illustrator, Eric Carle. Later, she took the stance of a mathematician. Several times she broke the flow and rhythm of her reading in order to count the animals on the page. "I know how many we did this time . . . one, two, three, four, five, six, seven." Shifts in stance like these offered Sarah new perspectives on her knowing (Harste et al. 1984) and deepened her understanding of language and story. In her reading she learned language (how to use it), learned about language (how to talk about it), and learned through language (how to find out about the world through it) (Halliday 1980).

These and similar examples in other readings show that Sarah was not imitating or reciting a memorized text. She brought to her reading all the knowledge and understanding about language and the world she had gained from her experiences. She was actively transacting with, thinking about, engaging in, critiquing, and processing text to construct meaning for herself. She intuitively understood the reading process and how it works and drew on everything she knew to use that process and read. Her reading contained all the elements of readings by proficient readers, with the exception of integrating graphophonic cues. As she gained experience, she gained greater control over the process and began to focus more on integrating print into her readings, not changing her reading process but orchestrating it more proficiently.

Sarah Invents How to Write

At one time I wouldn't have thought a young child capable of knowing anything of real importance about writing or the writing process. Again, Sarah challenged my beliefs. When at two and a half she wrote in written wavy lines and instructed, "Read this!" she reflected "a basic understanding of written marks as cultural objects which have a sign potential" (Harste et al. 1984, 108). Sarah's experiences observing others write for authentic purposes, using gestures to represent or enhance the meaning she was expressing, creating imaginary worlds in her play either alone or with Matthew or other children, and creating marks with her fingers by running them through sand, the carpet, and steam on the mirror all nurtured her under-standing that symbols in space or on a surface represent meaning and prompted her to reach for crayons and pencils (Fein 1993). Her writing grew as a distinct symbol system to represent meaning out of these experi-ences (Dyson 1989; Vygotsky 1983). She understood that writing allows us to share meaning with others in our society, and she used her knowledge of the semantic-pragmatic and syntactic language systems to communicate her meaning even though she could not yet control how to express that mean-ing graphically.

As soon as we returned from Montana that Christmas, Sarah, two years seven months, began writing copiously, using the knowledge she had of lan-guage to invent what she needed to express her meaning. The salient features of our English writing system are lines and circles (DeFord 1980), so she natu-rally perceived and used these to invent how to write, concentrating her atten-tion on understanding how we organize these shapes (Ferreiro 1990).

For several weeks Sarah continued to write only with lines, sometimes horizontal, sometimes vertical, reflecting the top-to-bottom and left-to-right organization of our language system. On one occasion, for example, she wrote three long vertical lines stretching almost from the top to the bottom of the page and announced, "It says 'people'." Children sometimes repre-sent physical characteristics of their topic graphically in their writing (Fer-reiro & Teberosky 1982), so we have reason to speculate on why Sarah invented how to write "people" with long lines. Because the writing in her environment includes more than one symbol, she used multiple lines in her writing. Her lines contrasted with her drawings made with continuous circu-lar motions, prompting me to refer to them as writing in our conversations. I regularly asked, What did you write? or What did you draw? depending on the surface features of her work. She never disputed or corrected my refer-ences. By referring to her work as writing (or drawing) I supported and deepened her understanding of what writing (or drawing) is and what its function is, and her view of herself as a capable writer (or artist). These con-cepts were shaped and enriched socially as they became more personally meaningful to her.

After several days of writing with lines, Sarah suddenly stopped writing completely. When I noticed this and asked her if she had written or was planning to write anything, she sadly and dejectedly responded, "I can't write. I don't know how." Despite my reassurance and encouragement, her insecurity with writing continued for several weeks. While she didn't verbalize her feelings and concerns, I suspect she realized from the print in her environment that there is more to our writing system than horizontal and vertical lines.

Sarah's reluctance to write did not carry over into a reluctance to draw, however. She continued to use markers, crayons, and pencils, concentrating on embedding meaning in her drawings and, over time, refining them by adding details and color.

The drawings in Figure 3-1 are representative of those reflecting Sarah's growth over the following three months. In contrast to her earlier creations formed by continuous repeated circular motions, her drawings became coordinated and controlled images, reflecting her understanding of the relationship between her art and the world (Cohen & Gainer 1995). The theme of her drawings was the portrait—of herself and other people important to her, primarily family members, and some of her favorite characters, including Baby Jesus, Mr. Rogers, and the Little Mermaid. Her portraits concentrated on the heads of her subjects. Since the head is the location of self, this is not surprising or unusual; the trunk, arms, or legs are never consistently used to represent a person (Lark-Horovitz, Lewis, & Luca 1967).

Initially Sarah's circles were open-ended. As she worked on learning to close them, she began adding facial details—eyes, mouth, a mark indicating hair—and sometimes also vertical marks to represent the beginnings of a body (see Figure 3-1-A). At two years nine months, when she eventually drew a closed circle, she began to embed more distinctive facial details in her portraits (see Figure 3-1-B). The wide downturned mouth was a characteristic of her portraits for awhile, not to indicate sadness but because that sweeping left-to-right stroke was an easy natural movement for her. Her intent was not to mirror reality but to use symbols to represent and communicate her meaning. This was a pivotal understanding for Sarah in her literacy learning. Realizing she could produce her own symbols to represent and communicate meaning laid the foundation for her understanding that she could represent meaning with her own symbols as well as give meaning to others' symbols (Cohen & Gainer 1995).

One day, after several months of not writing, I found Sarah, two years ten months, at the kitchen table, marker in hand, smiling proudly and working cheerfully . When I sat down and asked her what she was doing, she very

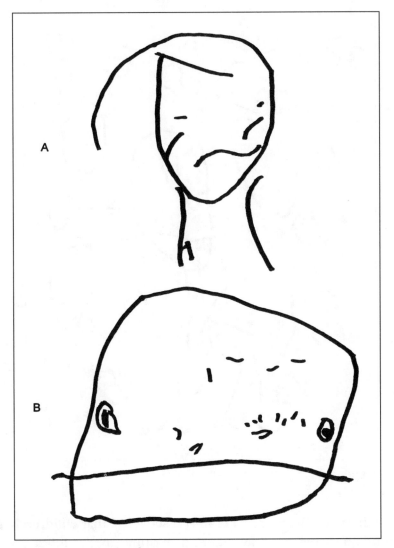

Figure 3-1. Sarah's first portraits.

matter-of-factly announced she had written <o>s [the symbol < > will be used to indicate the letter designated] and seemed surprised that I couldn't figure that out for myself. She had realized that the circle she had learned to use in her portraits could also function as an <o> in her writing (see Figure 3-2). Several features about both Sarah's drawing and her writing are

27

Figure 3-2. Sarah writes with <o>s.

noteworthy here. Emilia Ferreiro (1984) discovered that children beginning to differentiate between drawing and writing freely fill a page with graphemes with no linearity and little variety, limited only by the boundaries of the paper, as Sarah did here with her abundance of <o>s. To Sarah <o> was a letter, an object in the world like a table or a car, incapable of being or representing anything else. It, like any other object, went by the name we use to identify it, namely <o> (Ferreiro & Teberosky 1982).

While the portraits in her drawing are also circular, they are nevertheless very distinct from her <o>s. The dots and lines embedded in them unquestionably designate them as portraits. For the first time Sarah here included two portraits in one creation, one large and one small, perhaps an adult and a child. She distinguishes them in a number of ways: size, detail (the adult has hair, arms, and a wider mouth), and, in her original drawing, color.

Sarah had distinguished between drawing and writing several months earlier (see Figure 2-1), but she had never used <o>s to write until now. Whereas before she had written only with lines and drawn primarily with circles, she was now expanding and enriching her use of lines and circles, learning new functions for each, gaining confidence in herself, and understanding more about writing through art and about art through writing. When she perceived that she could use the same strokes (lines) and shapes (circles) for different purposes, depending on the meaning she wanted to represent, she enriched and expanded the potential of both her writing and her drawing and clarified for herself the unique function each has. Secure and confident in this enriched understanding, she wove her lines and circles together to draw and write in one created work. Sarah was actively making thoughtful complex decisions about how to organize and distinguish between her drawing and her writing (Harste et al. 1984).

With her lines and circles Sarah had the tools to write every alphabet in the world (Platt 1975) and draw anything she chose to represent. It was her immersion in rich literacy experiences in American society and culture that constrained her to situate her writing within the boundaries of our alphabetic English language.

Sarah's <o>s did not remain restricted to their role of "object in the world" for long. One afternoon when I wandered over to see what Sarah, then three years old, was working on at the kitchen table, there were no drawings with her "sentences" and she read me messages for what she had written (see Figure 3-3). Through her growing experience with written language, as she observed and participated in natural literacy events with others, Sarah had come to understand that writing is not composed of isolated "letters" but of symbols representing meaning. Her <o>s became placeholders for her meaning.

That understanding is a basic one for all readers and writers. Individual letters do not represent meaning; readers do not read letters. Readers use their knowledge and understanding to transact with symbols organized into a coherent text that represents meaning.

There is a noticeable reduction in the quantity of Sarah's <o>s between Figure 3-2 and Figure 3-3. Because she was inventing how to represent

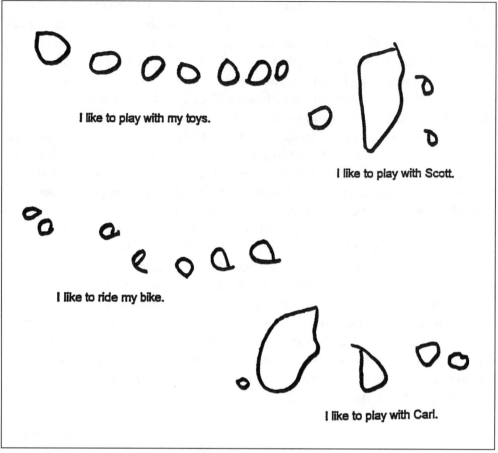

I like to play with my toys.

I like to play with Scott.

I like to ride my bike.

I like to play with Carl.

Figure 3-3. Sarah's <o>s are placeholders for her meaning.

meaning or to "say something" (Ferreiro 1984) with her <o>s, she naturally limited their number to roughly correspond to the boundaries of her message. Having earlier made and understood the distinction between drawing and writing, she now revisited and refined that knowledge, realizing that to write she does not "draw" letters but uses symbols to placehold her meaning. Perhaps her focus on written language explains at least in part why she chose not to include artwork as she usually did.

As a point of interest, Carl and Scott were neighborhood brothers several years older than Sarah, and thus considerably larger than she was.

Sarah's <o>s in all of her sentences are relatively the same size, with the exception of one <o> in each of the sentences about Carl and Scott. The larger <o> in each of these sentences probably reflects the physical characteristics of the subjects of these sentences.

In the months that followed, Sarah continued writing and drawing for her own pleasure and purposes, sometimes bringing her creations to me, other times leaving them scattered in the corners of her bedroom or elsewhere in the house. If I asked, she would often elaborate on her drawings, but rarely on her writing. In her art, she was better able to control more how to embed and represent her meaning. She was also beginning to realize that she could represent meaning in her art that she couldn't in her writing and vice versa.

Sarah's portraits usually had an arclike curved stroke toward the bottom of the figure that was probably meant to be arms or, more likely, the beginnings of a body. She included more complete bodies in the days to come and incorporated new symbols into her writings. These symbols resembled letters such as <a>, <t>, <h>, <w>, and <I>, indicating she was perceiving other features of the print in her environment. The organization she chose for her creations, with her writing above or below a drawing, reflected the familiar mainstream text/illustration organization in literature and in the environmental print in her community. By using that organization she elevated her work to the status of text and illustration and demonstrated her desire to participate and communicate meaning with others in her social environment (Harste et al. 1984).

Sarah as Songwriter

From birth Sarah had been growing as a symbolizer and socializer (Dyson 1989): a symbolizer able to represent objects or events with symbols or signs (Harste et al. 1984; Piaget 1970) and a socializer constructing meaning not alone but with others. As a symbolizer and socializer she was very aware that we have multiple ways of sharing meaning in our society. We daily hear or use math, music, play, movement, and art, for example, to communicate meaning in particular settings for particular purposes. Not surprising (although initially I was surprised, for the possibility had not occurred to me), Sarah, three years four months, invented other ways to represent meaning in addition to the writing and art we've seen so far. I began finding papers with rows of wavy lines (see Figure 3-4) around the house. At first I assumed they were her inventions of adult cursive writing, but when I asked, she referred to them as her "songwriter" and sang them to me. When I asked about the darkened spot at the end of the songwriting in Figure 3-4-A, Sarah explained, "That means stop," and drew a stop sign with an <s> to clarify

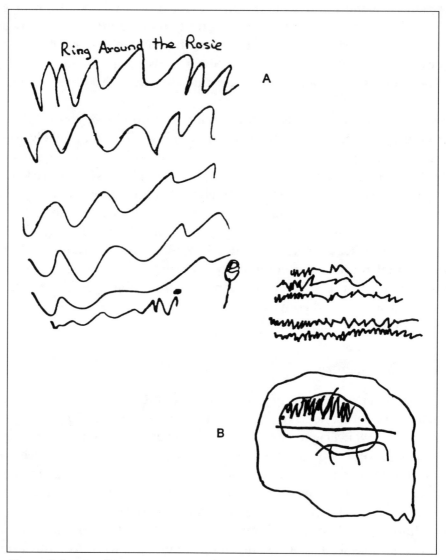

Figure 3-4. Sarah's songwriting.

and represent her symbolic message to the singer in another way. (Matthew was writing stories in first grade at this time, and on several occasions I had discussed the function of periods with him. Sarah had evidently overheard those conversations.) The songwriting in Figure 3-4-B, which I found on the floor of her bedroom, shares the page with a portrait. I do not know whether the figure and the songwriting are related or whether the circle around the portrait is meant to be a boundary separating it from the song-writing. In either case, the surface features here and in her written language texts demonstrate Sarah's understanding that meanings in music and in art are represented differently from each other and are in turn different from meaning represented in written language. She knows that each has its own strengths depending on the function and purpose of the meaning she is rep-resenting. Because the functions and purposes differ, she invents different forms or surface texts for each (Harste et al. 1984).

I suspect Sarah invented her songwriting with wavy lines to reflect the flow of the melody when we sing. I'm not sure what prompted this inven-tion. She observed her family and friends sing from hymnals in church, heard music being sung occasionally on television or the radio, and enjoyed singing herself, but music was not a central part of our family life. We did not even own a stereo, record player, or piano at the time. Sarah actively contin-ued her songwriting for months. At home she'd songwrite and sing familiar songs; in church she would create her songwriting and pass copies out to Ray, Matthew, and me when we sang, or hold and sing from them herself to participate in the service. When her songwriting had served its purpose for her, it disappeared from her inventions.

Sarah Invents the Syllabic Hypothesis

Before school one morning Matthew, six and a half, was sitting at the kitchen table making a birthday card for his teacher. Not wanting to be excluded from the fun, Sarah, three years four months, quickly crawled up on another chair to join in. She picked up a marker and set to work while Matthew and I conversed about his day and what he needed to remember to do. Shortly thereafter Sarah set down her marker and showed us what she had created. Her paper contained no art, only four symbols resembling <I>s each with a number of extra parallel cross marks (similar to the symbols in Figure 3-5-A).

Sarah proudly pointed and read, "Hap-py Birth-day," matching each syllable she spoke with a separate symbol she had written.

Emilia Ferreiro (1984; Ferreiro & Teberosky 1982) refers to this "matching" of oral words or syllables with written marks as the syllabic hypothesis. The syllabic hypothesis is a "guess" children invent for how to relate the language they speak and hear with the language they read and write in texts. Sarah's writing made sense (the semantic-pragmatic system) and sounded like language (the syntactic system). With the syllabic hypothesis she invented how to integrate the third language system, the graphophonic system, into her writing. The syllabic hypothesis marks the beginning of children's understanding of phonics, of the relationship between oral and written language: they learn the criteria for limiting the number of letters and focus their attention on how letter patterns relate to sound patterns, even though they may not yet understand the alphabetic principle (Ferreiro 1991; K. Goodman 1993).

Applying the Syllabic Hypothesis to Writing

For the next two weeks Sarah used the syllabic hypothesis whenever she wrote, be it for her own enjoyment, in play with Matthew, or for a specific purpose such as making a card for a grandparent. (For examples, see Figure 3-5.)

Sarah's creations usually contained a picture or portrait that she drew first, accompanied by writing (as in Figure 3-5-A). Sometimes she chose only to write (as in Figure 3-5-B). Occasionally she wrote with an assortment of symbols, but usually her symbols were repetitive and showed little variation.

Many children use the letters of their names when they write (Harste et al. 1984). Sarah displayed no interest in writing her name and thus chose other letters. She basically restricted herself to <I> and <T>, even though she recognized and had written other letters before this time. She also was content to write with a string of identical letters, not concerned with the lack of internal variation.

In our English writing system we rarely have patterns of more than two identical letters in succession. Ferreiro and Teberosky (1982) found that many children believe that for print to be readable it must contain two to four, generally three, letters and these letters cannot be repeated more

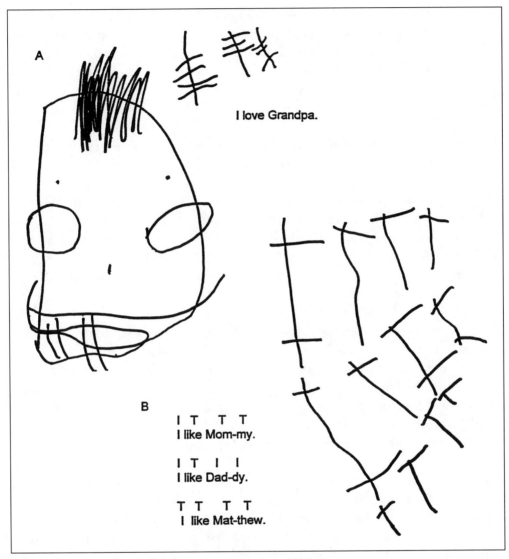

I love Grandpa.

I T T T
I like Mom-my.

I T I I
I like Dad-dy.

T T T T
I like Mat-thew.

Figure 3-5. Sarah writes with the syllabic hypothesis.

than three times. Children decide this based on their transactions with print in their environment. Sarah was concerned about the number of letters in her writing inventions (she usually wrote at least three symbols) but not with the prominent variation between the letters. I believe she limited

35

herself to <I> and <T> because those were easy to write and did not distract her from her primary goal of creating meaning and understanding how written language, oral language, and meaning are related. Surface features of her text, how her text "looked," were not as important to her as the deeper meaning she wanted to communicate. However, in Figure 3-5-B there is variation *between* sentences, distinguishing between the different meanings in each.

Three other aspects of Sarah's inventions are worth noting at this point. First, she was continuing to embed more detail and meaning in her art and to refine her understanding of art as a sign system. She curved the mouth of her portrait into an upward smile, added more hair to the top of the head and added ears to the face, and drew dimensional legs. Her art was also expanding in other ways not illustrated here. For example, the curved arclike stroke that had earlier represented a body she expanded in a different setting into a rainbow, using concentric arcs and even adding some color to make her drawing more authentic. She also sometimes added earrings to her figures as well as feet to the legs.

As she embedded more meaning in her art, Sarah also defined her understanding of art and its function. It is significant that in connection with three pivotal "firsts" in her understanding of written language *no* art was involved at all: her first wavy lines and "Read this!" request; her <o>s becoming placeholders for her meaning; and her oral match of the four syllables of Happy Birthday with four written symbols. While it can be argued that her attention and concentration were focused on aspects of written language at those times, Sarah was also growing in her understanding that different sign systems, such as art, music, written language, math, and so on, represent meaning differently. The sign system chosen affects the meaning expressed; and the intended meaning constrains the choice of sign systems. The meaning Sarah wanted to communicate in these instances was best represented in written language. While other sign systems were available to her, she understood that she could not represent her meaning as clearly or succinctly in any other than written language. As she distinguished between the function and purpose of drawing and writing, she distinguished between the function and purpose of different sign systems.

Second, through her continuing experiences with written language Sarah also knew that some aspects of language are relatively stable and some vary. The spellings of words, for example, are standard but we vary word order in a sentence to express meaning. We can even express the same meaning in different ways. *My favorite color is blue* and *Blue is my favorite color* are different surface structures representing the same meaning. Sorting through and distinguishing between which aspects are stable and which vary, Sarah experimented with and invented new forms of letters. Her <I>s in Figure 3-5-A are an example of her experimenting with how many cross lines she can add and still have an <I>.

Finally, Sarah used the sentence starter *I love* or *I like* for virtually all her writing, other than names, for about five months. In one sense this form constrained and restricted her written language at a time when her oral language was rapidly expanding. In another sense, though, her sentence starter was liberating. As with her use of <I> and <T>, it released her to concentrate on aspects of our language system on which she chose to focus. *I love/like* was a syntactic structure that provided her with a theme and format to express herself and represent who she was (Rowe 1987), changing the specific content depending on her semantic-pragmatic purposes. Her sentence starter is an example of the "workbook" exercise Glenda Bissex (1984) suggests children sometimes organize for themselves as they search for the rules governing language.

The power of Sarah's sentence starter for her literacy came from her inventing it for herself as a means of learning how written language works. She knew better than anyone else what she wanted and needed to know and how she could best learn it. This was intuitive on her part, not something she could verbally express. Had I imposed that sentence structure on her, it would have inhibited, restricted, and disenfranchised her.

Following two weeks of this strict one-to-one correspondence between her oral words/syllables and her written text to represent her meaning, Sarah, three years five months, suddenly began incorporating more letters into her written inventions, including her invented forms of the lowercase <a> and <h> she saw in her name (although she still showed no interest in writing her name), and elongating one sound in her spoken sentence to match her extended written text (examples are included in Figure 3-6).

Perhaps Sarah added more and new letters to her writing because she was perceiving the writing in her environment in more detail and noticed

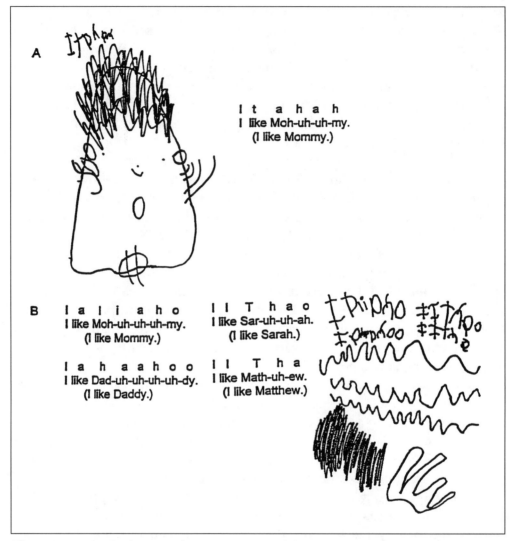

Figure 3-6. Sarah elongates her voice to match her writing.

it was longer than the three to five letters she typically wrote with little variation in the letters. Perhaps she felt confident with the one-to-one syllabic relationship of written language, oral language, and meaning and wanted to understand how to hear specific sound patterns and relate them to specific letter patterns. Or perhaps she enjoyed confidently generating more involved meaning and wanted to write it as she saw family members and others in her community do. For whatever reason, her writing inventions became more detailed and demonstrated more variation in the letters.

The creation in Figure 3-6-B is particularly interesting since Sarah again invents how to represent meaning in different sign systems. In written language, she writes four sentences, varying the internal sequence of letters in each to represent the different meaning of each. In music she uses her songwriting. In art, for the first time, she draws an aspect of nature, grass, as well as part of her body, the part she often uses to create meaning in other sign systems, her hand. Sarah drew or traced her handprint on her work many times in the months to follow. Her handprints became another theme she used as a "signature" or "logo" to represent or sign her individuality in the world.

Sarah's portrait drawings became more detailed. Virtually overnight she moved from awkward rough sketches, as in Figure 3-5-A, to more mature, elaborate, precise drawings, as in Figure 3-6-A. The smiling mouths became more proportional and contained within the face. She added arms or fingers, smaller ears, and included more hair to cover the heads. The small circle just under the smile in Figure 3-6-A she said was a belly button. In other drawings she occasionally included other body parts, such as knees.

As Sarah gained experience, she became more attentive to the finer aspects of language and her world. Her perceptions, and thus her inventions, reflected more of the details around her and she refined her inventions of written language as well as her drawings to represent her meanings more precisely.

Applying the Syllabic Hypothesis to Reading

Simultaneous with inventing and exploring the syllabic hypothesis in her writing, Sarah invented and explored it in her reading to understand the mysterious relationship between the language and meaning she heard and the written text she saw. At three years of age she displayed a keen understanding of the interrelationship of reading and writing. In contrast to her writing, though, in inventing the syllabic hypothesis in reading she began by elongating her voice to match the print and moved to a one-to-one correspondence between what she read and symbols in the text.

The first time I noticed Sarah make a connection between her oral language, meaning, and the written text, she was reading *Hattie and the Fox* (Fox 1986). In the story a fox sneaks into the farmyard and is scared away by the cow. When Sarah came to the page of text that read, "But the cow said, 'MOO!' so loudly that the fox was frightened and ran away," she pointed to that line of text but read, "The cow said, 'MOO!' and the fox ran aaaaaaaaaway." She did not stop vocalizing "aaaaaaaaaway" until her finger reached the end of the printed sentence. She knew that oral language, written language, and meaning are related and invented a way to show the relationship.

This was the only instance I heard Sarah elongating her voice when she read literature to match her oral meaning with the written text. After this, she began exploring the syllabic hypothesis in reading by matching an oral word or syllable with a written letter, similar to how she invented this relationship in her writing. For example:

- Sarah, three years four months, was reading *Time for School, Little Dinosaur* (Herman 1990). On one page is a picture of a bus stop with a sign reading *BUS*. When she turned to this page Sarah said, "I know what that says [referring to the sign]. Bus [pointing to the <B>], Bus [pointing to the <U>], Bus [pointing to the <S>]."

- Sarah, three years four months, picked up *The Wheels of the Bus* (Ziefert 1990) to read. She told me she could read the title and said *Bus* as she pointed to each letter of each word in the title (with a definite perplexed look on her face as she continued repeating *Bus*).

- On one page of *The Stupids Die* (Allard 1981) the clock bongs eleven times. Sarah, three years five months, was reading the book and when she came to that part of the story she pointed to each *letter* of the first six *bong*s, which were all on one line, and read *bong*. When that didn't seem right to her, she pointed to each word and read *bong* for the last five *bong*s on the next line.

- Sarah and I were reading *Goodnight Owl* (Hutchins 1972). I pointed out the word *owl* on one page. On the next page Sarah found *owl* herself, then pointed to the <o> in *to* on another line and said, "There's *owl* too."

As Sarah invented how to represent her meaning in her writing by matching one oral word or syllable with one written symbol, she invented how to match one written symbol with one oral word or syllable in her reading. Through her growing experience with reading and writing she would refine her one-to-one hypothesis of the relationship between oral language, written language, and meaning to understand how patterns of letters, patterns of sounds, syntactic structure, and meaning relate.

Refining Writing

For about one week Sarah again changed her hypothesis and thus the focus of her inventions of written language. Instead of repeating the same sound in her elongation of her text as in Figure 3-6, she singled out and tried to hear the particular sounds in one word. For example, she wrote five symbols and read "I like Luh-oo-ke" ("I like Luke") and she wrote seven symbols and read "I like the ss-nn-ow-wuh" ("I like the snow"). With this invention the difference in her art and writing from days before was marked: she reverted to using little variation in the letters she chose, repeating the same letters and relying primarily on <I> and <T>; and her drawing became less detailed and more simplified and sketchy. As it turned out, Sarah was on the verge of a major discovery and understanding about written language. The happenings of the next few days and weeks were pivotal to her literacy learning. Perhaps that was why she again focused less on surface features and more on how oral language meaning and written language meaning are related.

Sarah as Reader and Writer

While Sarah's inventions in this chapter of how oral meanings relate to written text do not completely "work," they indicate her growing understanding that there is more to reading than producing a meaningful response to a book and more to writing than making marks on paper. She intuitively used her knowledge of language systems in her inventions because they are intrinsic to language and language learning. Her grasp of the syntactic and semantic-pragmatic systems of language is evident: her stories, whether she was reading or writing, made sense (the semantic-pragmatic system) and sounded like language (the syntactic system). She had less of a grasp on integrating print into her reading and writing (the graphophonic system). But that was about to change.

4

"How Do We Read and Write?"

During the year after Sarah wrote her wavy lines on paper and requested, "Read this!" she continued to research her inquiries into "What are *you* doing with that written language?" "How can *I* read and write?" and "How do *we* read and write?" Not only did she observe and participate with others reading and writing for countless purposes in a variety of contexts, but she continually invented and refined how to read and write herself, based on her knowledge and growing experience. She read books, signs, labels, and other texts, as well as her own writing, including genres such as thank-you notes, birthday cards, and *I like/love* personal narratives.

Intrinsic to her inventions and how she used written language was an awareness that written language has "rules" that facilitate our sharing meaning with each other. She had learned about these "rules" (reading and writing from left to right on a page, writing alphabet letters to create words, using periods as punctuation, and so on) naturally, because they are integral to the written language of our society and culture. Of course Sarah did not fully understand and control these "rules" and her reading and writing were by no means "conventional," because she did not integrate all three language systems proficiently. Nevertheless, the more I observed her, talked with her, and discovered the depth and sophistication of her thinking and understanding, even as a three-year-old, the more impressed I became with the power, authenticity, and legitimacy of her literacy.

Two significant literacy experiences—learning to write her name and discovering the alphabetic principle—within three weeks of each other challenged and encouraged Sarah to refine her inventions. While still exploring what we "do" with written language and how she could read and write, she intensified her inquiry into "How do *we* read and write?"

Sarah Writes Her Name

For some children, learning to write their name is their first order of business when they begin creating meaning through writing. This was not true for Sarah. In contrast to her intense interest and desire to understand and generate other writing, she displayed *no* interest or desire in learning to write her name. She spent her days at home, usually with her father, playing, visiting, reading, drawing, writing, running errands, or watching TV. The written language in her environment always served a specific, authentic function and purpose. She had no authentic function and purpose for writing her name.

Then, at three and a half, three weeks before Christmas, Sarah entered preschool. She came home from her first day excited about her new friends and everything she had experienced and with a dramatic sense of urgency, she let us know that she *had* to know how to spell and write *Sarah* immediately not because the school insisted but because she made up her mind it was time to learn. No doubt seeing her new friends writing their names and finding her classmates' names on coat hooks, cubbies, papers, and lunch boxes was the catalyst that ignited her interest. The function, purpose, and need for writing her name had become explicitly evident.

Before she would write her name, Sarah was adamant that she first learn to spell it. So, for the next several days she practiced spelling *S-a-r-a-h* out loud and finding those letters on signs, candy wrappers, menus, Sunday School pamphlets, anything and everything. Almost a week later, only when she felt confident with the spelling, did she pick up a marker to write. (It didn't occur to me at the time that helping her spell her name correctly contrasted with the inventing she did in her other writing.)

Sarah used an upper case <S> but otherwise wrote lowercase letters at my direction. Her play with the positioning of the letters was noticeable. Positioning letters in their appropriate direction is not a simple concept for children to perceive, understand, and produce conventionally. While our writing system moves left to right, many letters are formed by moving right to left, depending on the conventional shape and direction of the letter and where the writer chooses to begin writing: top right, top left, lower right, or lower left. In *Sarah*, the <S> is formed beginning at the top right and moving to top left and snaking around. The <a> conventionally faces from right to left and is often formed by making the circle first, moving right to left. Both <r> and <h> face from left to right and are formed by moving in a left-to-right direction.

In light of these complexities, it is not surprising that Sarah, on her own, without any interference, experimented with writing her name (see Figure 4-1-A). For the first three weeks she positioned her <S> conventionally about half the time and the other half wrote it "backwards." Backwards from my point of view, however, was not backwards from hers, since her backward <S> in effect moved left to right, as does our writing system. She had a lot to remember: write her name across the page from left to right but form the first letter in it by moving right to left. Her <a>s were always backward, which again only meant facing left to right. To form her <a> Sarah made the circle first moving left to right, lifted her pencil, and then attached the stick on the left side of the circle. The <r> she positioned conventionally (left to right), and the <h> she left "uncommitted" (drawing the hump first and placing the stick up from the middle of the hump). In other words, Sarah both wrote her name and positioned the letters in her name to face left to right, experimenting half the time with the direction of the <S>.

Then, for about four days, Sarah often faced her <S> conventionally but positioned her name backward, or right to left (following the right-to-left direction of her <S>), the rest of the letters remaining unchanged (see Figure 4-1-B). After those four days, she never reversed her entire name again, but her <S> was consistently backward (see Figure 4-1-C). A few days later she flipped her <a> and <r>, the <a> now facing conventionally but the <r> positioned backward (see Figure 4-1-D).

Figure 4-1. Sarah learns to write her name.

The positioning in Figure 4-1-D remained her signature for a year, at which point she suddenly decided to shift to all uppercase letters, as we'll see later. While she sometimes intermixed upper- and lowercase letters in her other writing, she never did in her name.

Once Sarah knew how to write her own name, she worked intensely over the next several weeks on learning to write *Matthew*, *Mommy*, and *Daddy*. These names, as well as her own name, were the most personal and meaningful writings Sarah had produced, and the only writing she learned and wrote conventionally and did not invent. These names, along with the names of her friends at preschool, made her keenly aware, as no other writing had, that we as a society have specific ways of spelling specific words. Specific letter patterns represent specific sound patterns, quite unlike the writing system she had invented of using one letter (with little variety in the letters she used) per word, syllable, or elongated sound to represent her meaning.

Sarah Discovers the Alphabetic Principle

Two weeks after learning to write her name Sarah, three years six months, had another pivotal literacy experience that challenged her to think and consider more critically the writing system she had invented. She was writing a thank-you note for a Christmas gift. After drawing a picture she told me she was going to write *I love you*. She had been using her *I love/like* personal sentence starter for over a year, but this was the first time she wanted to write *I love you*. After writing *I*, Sarah looked up at me:

Sarah: I know what says *luh, luh, luh*.
Prisca: What.
Sarah: <L> goes *luh*.
Prisca: How do you know?
Sarah: Because *luh* for *love*.

With that she wrote <L> next to her I, followed by an inverted <U>. When she finished, the enlightened astonishment on her face as she looked from her paper to me and back to her paper told me she understood how our written language system relates to oral language meaning, namely, through the alphabetic principle. In that "developmental moment" (Whitmore 1992; Whitmore & Y. Goodman 1995) she began to understand how written language makes sense (Y. Goodman 1984). She also realized she needed to refine her personal inventions to situate them within the context of the written language system of her community so she could share her meaning with others and they could share theirs with her. ILU, representing I love you, became an integral and regular part of Sarah's signature for months to come.

The weeks that followed this discovery were not easy for Sarah. She was comprehending *how* reading is more than producing a meaningful story in response to a book and *how* writing is more than making marks on paper to represent her meaning. She was intuitively, not consciously, aware that she needed to integrate the graphophonic system with the semantic-pragmatic and syntactic systems—and she knew she didn't know how. The chasm between what she discerned "should be" in her reading and writing and what she "could do" rocked her confidence and created a major disequilibrium. Overwhelmed by what she was aware she didn't know, things "fell apart" (Goodman 1993) for Sarah. She was consciously aware that the system she had invented for written language was not "right" and did not "work" in the real world. The new perceptions and insights she was gaining into her knowledge and understanding would, in the weeks to come, refine and propel her literacy.

Over the next days and weeks Sarah became more and more reluctant to read or write. Her facial expressions were tense and concerned and her mannerisms stiff and controlled anytime she encountered books or writing materials. In reading, holistic remembering no longer "counted." Many books she was unwilling even to attempt to read herself. In those she did select she was very concerned with the exact wording, which she hadn't been before, and would ask, How does it go? or What does it say right here? She still gravitated toward certain old favorites, though, such as *The Gingerbread Man* (Martin 1990) and *Are You My Mommy?* (Dijs 1990), and read them confidently, using the refrains and text like *I*, *me*, *Mommy*, and *no* as her "landmarks" to guide her when she chose to follow the print with her finger. Building on the knowledge and understanding she had, she worked to refine her timing so she would be reading the landmark portion of text at the moment her finger reached it. I continued to support and encourage but not push her. I read to her and partner-read with her to keep her immersed in the richness of language and literature and allow her to experience all of the language systems working in concert. After several weeks she regained her confidence and freely read on her own again, but she was more conscious of the print and of examining it closely.

The disequilibrium Sarah experienced in writing was more difficult for her to resolve. She was highly reluctant to write and much less prolific. When she did write, though, she no longer elongated sounds as she had just days before (Figure 3-6), but wrote syllabic-alphabetically, representing a prominent sound in each word or syllable with an appropriate letter and inserting a placeholder when she was unsure of what to write.

The example in Figure 4-2 is representative of Sarah's writing at this

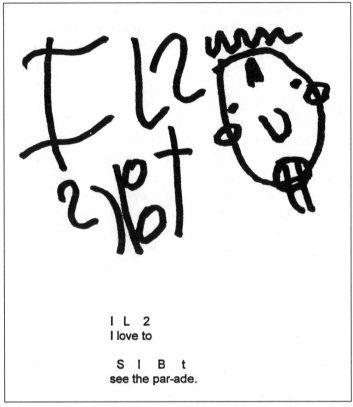

I L   2
I love to

S I B   t
see the par-ade.

Figure 4-2. Sarah writes with the syllabic-alphabetic hypothesis.

time. Here, as in her other writing, she represents *I* with <I> and *love* with <L> because *love* begins with /l/. She uses the numeral *2* to represent *to*, <s> to represent *see* (because see begins with /s/), and a placeholder to represent *the*. She represented *par-ade* with *B t* because /p/ (voiceless phoneme) and /b/ (voiced phoneme) as well as /d/ (voiced phoneme) and /t/ (voiceless phoneme) are articulated similarly.

Gradually, though, even with support and encouragement, Sarah's hesitation and reluctance to write escalated until finally for a couple weeks she would not write at all. If I suggested writing or encouraged her, she would say, "I can't write," "I don't know how," or "I don't want to write." She was paralyzed by what she perceived as her own inadequacy and lack of knowledge of how to write "correctly," not unlike what happens to some children and adults who focus so much, so soon, on convention and accuracy that they lose sight of the purpose of reading and writing, namely to construct and share meaning.

Sarah's Placeholder "Stick"

For Valentine's Day Matthew and Sarah received money as gifts, and I suggested they each write a thank-you note. Matthew wrote his note immediately, but Sarah refused. Over the next few days I periodically repeated my suggestion, but when Sarah didn't express any interest I dropped the subject.

One afternoon she voluntarily came to me, announced she wanted to write her thank-you note, and asked me to sit with her while she worked. She first drew a picture and then stated, "I'm going to write, Thank you for the money." Since this was the first writing she had done in weeks, I was at once relieved, excited, and curious. She began by saying "Thank," paused briefly without writing anything, then went on, simultaneously saying and writing "you for" as *U 4*. Then she paused, looked up at me, and asked, "Mommy, how do you write *the*?" In the split second that followed I realized that if I "helped" her by spelling *t-h-e*, a one-syllable word with two phonemes and three letters, I would only add to the disequilibrium she was trying to resolve. I thought fast:

Prisca: You know, Sarah, sometimes when I'm writing I'm not sure what to put down, and you want to know what I do when that happens?
Sarah: What.
Prisca: I put in a line and keep going. That way I know something goes there and can come back and fix it later but can keep writing now.
Sarah: Oh.

With that she used <I> as her "stick" (she interpreted *line* as *stick*) to represent *the* and *thank* and continued, writing *m e* for *mon-ey*, representing the prominent sound she heard in each syllable.

Placeholders were not new for Sarah. She had used <o>s as placeholders, had invented "stick" placeholders herself a few weeks earlier (see Figure 4-2), and used verbal placeholders in her holistic remembering of stories and responses to other print. She just needed to be reminded of and given permission to use them now that she was understanding in more depth and intricacy how our written language system works.

Sarah's placeholder "stick" gave her a strategy to use when she was unsure of and insecure about what to write. Spelling *t-h-e* for her would have been a one-time quick-fix solution that focused her attention on conventions and accuracy at a time when she needed a strategy to keep her focused on the purpose of writing: to create, represent, and share meaning. Conventional spellings are certainly important if we are to share meaning easily. I wanted Sarah to understand, though, that correct spelling was not intended to and should not inhibit, deter, or stop the creation of meaning. Besides, I reasoned that if inserting placeholders is a strategy I and other writers use, why not share it writer to writer, even with a three-year-old, rather than expect something of a child I don't always do as an adult—namely, to spell correctly in first drafts. Sarah has never hesitated to write or said *I can't* since that day.

Throughout this time Sarah was also refining and expanding her art and how she embedded meaning in it. Her figures usually had arms, legs, and bodies; hair covered the entire head; and many figures had eyebrows and proportional ears. She often drew several figures together, rather than only one, indicating an awareness of her social world. She also drew animals; placed "lipstick" on the lips and glasses on the eyes of her figures; decorated the page with borders; and represented arms and hands in different ways. Her continuous use of enlarged heads indicates her positive self-image and confidence as well as her understanding that the head is our center of awareness (Lark-Horovitz et al. 1967).

For several weeks Sarah exploited her discovery of her placeholder by including *Thank you for the money* in virtually everything she wrote or drew, even when it wasn't a thank-you note. In other writing she continued to write syllabic-alphabetically, using her placeholder—usually <i> or <I> —whenever she was unsure about how to represent a syllable or word.

Sarah used her "stick" placeholder for about four months, until she no longer needed it in that formalized way. It had served its purpose of showing her that "not knowing" does not and should not prevent her from writing her meaning and inventing how to share it with others. Sarah's "stick" continues to live on informally to this day, though. Every time she spells, writes, reads, draws, or creates with a central focus on making meaning, without allowing correctness and convention to inhibit or paralyze her, the power of her placeholder is evident.

Refining Writing Through Names

Sarah's *I love/like* theme disappeared about this time, perhaps because she was tired of it or didn't need it, perhaps because her "stick" was a new strategy to provide her with freedom to generate her meaning, perhaps because she had entered preschool and was now more "sophisticated" and "grown-up." Names became her new focus. She knew how to spell her own and her family members' names and turned her attention to her friends' names. In the months to follow, names played a significant and powerful role in helping Sarah refine her literacy.

Sarah thoroughly enjoyed preschool. While some time was spent on letters and sounds, the majority of the day by far was devoted to play, reading, art, and other activities that encouraged the children's creative and social development. Thrust into this thriving social life Sarah began writing list after list of her friends' names, sometimes just to identify them and sometimes specifically planning who she wanted to invite to her birthday party, which was still several months away. It was in these lists that she began moving beyond writing syllabic-alphabetically to writing names in more detail. Seeing her friends' names at school and observing them write their names with more than one, two, or three letters to represent the corresponding number of syllables no doubt encouraged Sarah to analyze the names and syllables in more depth (Ferreiro 1980).

The names in Figure 4-3 are a compilation taken from innumerable lists written at home over a six-month period. Sarah initially represented *Bianca*, a three-syllable name, with three letters, <B> and two placeholders. Over time she started to represent it with four letters, the <P> because of the articulatory similarity between /B/ and /P/, two placeholders, and <A>, probably because of the graphic influence of remembering Bianca has <A>s in her name. In *Katie*, Sarah moved from *Kb* (<b> is a <d> positioned left to right), each letter representing the letter name she heard as she pronounced each syllable (*Kay-dee*), to *KAb*, in which she represented the /K/ and /ey/ phonemes individually.

Figure 4-3. A compilation of names demonstrating Sarah's progress beyond the syllabic-alphabetic hypothesis.

Chelsea, a two-syllable name, Sarah moved from writing with three letters to four. The <T> represented <Ch> because the corresponding sounds are articulated similarly with the tongue at the upper gums. The second syllable, *-sea*, sounded like <C> to her initially so she represented it with <C>. As she gained experience, though, she used <C> to represent the /s/ she heard (because the letter name <C> begins with /s/) and added <e> to represent the /iy/ she heard. I suspect the <C> and <e> were also graphically influenced: Sarah knew she had seen those letters in Chelsea's name.

Jesse, *David*, and *Alex* are all two-syllable names Sarah represented with more than two letters. In *Alex* the influence of the graphic symbols she sees in his name is again evident. She spelled it *ALXS* as she pronounced it. However, she knew she had seen <e> in his name and tacked that on the end, a common place to find <e> in English, to produce *ALXSe*. *Belinda* is a three-syllable name she spelled with four letters, representing the prominent sounds she pronounced and again interchanging <B> and <P>.

Sarah did very little writing other than her name lists for these six months. She never asked how to spell a specific name and rarely asked if the name she had written was "correct." She was happy and content to write list after list. Her experiences with these names helped her understand that the syllable is not *the* unit of analysis in written language as it was in her syllabic hypothesis but may be broken into smaller elements (Ferreiro 1991).

Refining the Graphophonic System

The more Sarah used written language for authentic, functional purposes, the more experience she gained with it. And as she gained experience, she perceived finer and finer details of written language and invented how those aspects worked in her writing. She continually refined her inventions as she focused more on integrating the graphophonic system—the sound system (phonology), the graphic system (orthography), and the system that relates the two (phonics) (K. Goodman 1993)—with the semantic-pragmatic and syntactic systems of language.

Two major aspects of written language on which Sarah focused were spelling and punctuation, both of which were influenced by her experiences with children's literature. Sarah's boldness in taking risks to invent spelling and punctuation and to refine those inventions as she gained more experience propelled not only her own learning but mine as well.

Integrating the Graphophonic System into Writing

Learning to spell is a lifelong process. Sarah, like all children, began this process as an aspect of her literacy when she first noticed print and later made her first marks on paper. With these marks she was inventing a graphic way to represent her meaning, doing so long before she entered school and participated in any formal spelling program. Her invention of the syllabic hypothesis (Figure 3-5) more specifically focused her on phonics. Ken Goodman, in his book *Phonics Phacts* (1993), describes this learning process:

> Word and syllabic inventions are the beginning of phonics, even though the children don't yet understand the alphabetic principle: that letter patterns relate to sound patterns (not individual letters to individual sounds). Eventually, as they continue to try to make sense of written language, young readers and writers discover this principle and begin to do two things:
>
> • They remember what written words look like.
> • They develop their own rules for how the spellings relate to how the words sound.
>
> As in all language learning, they overgeneralize the rules at first. (p. 71)

We have seen in previous figures, especially in Figure 4-3, that as Sarah refined her written language inventions she incorporated the phonic system of rules into her sense of the graphic system, relating the orthography and her own phonology (K. Goodman 1993). With her revolutionizing awareness in writing *ILU*, and perhaps somewhat before, Sarah understood there is a system to written language and invented her own system for relating letter patterns and sound patterns. Because she expected language to be logical and make sense within the context of her world, her spelling inventions, although not conventional, were systematic and logical in her invented system.

Sarah's Phonics   For most of the years I taught in primary classrooms I thought of phonics as a relatively simple one-to-one relationship between letters and sounds. If I could teach my students those relationships they would be able to decode print and read and write. Children having difficulty reading and writing just needed more work with these letter/sound relationships.

I considered invented spelling to be a temporary part of the move toward correct and accurate spelling but didn't look for evidence of children's strengths or appreciate their knowledge revealed through invented spelling. And I certainly didn't consider that young children could be inventing spelling in a logical and systematic way unless I could read what they wrote.

As I studied Sarah's literacy I realized that she was not only inventing how to read and write but also inventing her own personal system of phonics.

She refined and grew in her understanding of phonics and how it works in reading and writing, making her system and her spelling more "conventional" within the context of her own reading and writing for her own meaningful purposes.

Sarah, like all children, invented how to write the significant phonemes she heard based on how she perceived the sounds (K. Goodman 1993). Perception occurs in our brains, not in our ears. We are very proficient at hearing sounds as if they are the same that in actuality are very different. One example is listening to speakers of different dialects pronounce the same words: the speakers sound different, but we understand them as saying the same thing. We are also proficient at treating sounds that are basically the same as different: *I will* meet *you after school* and *I had* meat *for dinner*. The homophones sound the same but we know they have different meanings. How a speaker pronounces a particular sound depends on the sounds preceding and following it. And, the particular contexts of sounds and words influence how the listener perceives them (K. Goodman 1993).

Charles Read (1971), in his research on preschool children's knowledge and categorization of speech sounds, found that as children perceive sounds they draw on conventional information such as the letter name, the sound of the letter name, and the place the sound, voiced or voiceless, is articulated in the mouth. Similarly articulated sounds include those made by placing the lips together, as with /p/ (voiceless) and /b/ (voiced); positioning the tip of the tongue at the upper gums, as with /t/ (voiceless) and /d/ (voiced); and positioning the tip of the tongue at the soft palate, as with /k/ (voiceless) and /g/ (voiced). How the child initially perceives sound patterns in a given context determines the graphic representation the child invents for these sound patterns in writing. These strategies are logical and reflect the child's own phonology and knowledge (K. Goodman 1993; Read 1971).

We have seen some of this in Sarah's spelling already. For example:

- She spelled using letter names: <u> for *you*, <e> in *money*, and <C> in *Chelsea*.
- She spelled using the sound of a letter name: <m> for /m/, <L> for /l/, <S> for /s/, <K> for /k/, and <v> for /v/.

- She spelled using a similar place of articulation for phonemes, interchanging /b/ and /p/, /t/ and /d/, /t/ and /ch/, and /k/ and /g/.

As Sarah's experience with written language grew and she refined her understanding, her perception of sounds continued to influence her spelling inventions. Other major sound perceptions, governed by her own pronunciation or phonology, appeared consistently in her writing.

One example is Sarah's perception and pronunciation of the <th> letter combination and its sound patterns. In English *thank* and *the* graphically begin with the same letter pattern, <th>, even though the sound patterns differ. Sarah perceived these different sound patterns as the same and pronounced them like /f/ as in finger. For example, she pronounced Matthew as *Ma-few* and three as *free*. Because /f/ is articulated in the front of the mouth by the teeth and lips, as /v/ is, Sarah represented the <t> pattern in her writing with <v>. Sarah was highly consistent with this spelling pattern for over a year until she learned, through her continued reading and writing, the conventional spelling pattern for the two different sound patterns.

Another sound Sarah represented in writing based on how she perceived and pronounced it was /r/. With the exception of some medial and final positions, she pronounced /r/ as /w/. For example, Terri she pronounced as *Te-wee* and Sarah as *Sa-wah*. Because the /w/ she pronounced sounds similar to the beginning of the letter name <Y>, she represented /r/ in her writing with <Y>.

Figure 4-4 is a thank-you note Sarah wrote to a member of the Phoenix Suns organization for basketball tickets our family had received. Sarah pronounced gorilla as *gowilla*, thus the <Y> representing /r/ in that spelling. The <Y> at the end of *Dear*, a fairly common but not consistent spelling for Sarah, has a similar explanation. When she pronounced *Dear* she sometimes produced an aspiration, or burst of air similar to the burst of air in /w/, prompting the <Y>. Because /g/ and /k/ are articulated similarly she begins *gorilla* with <k>. Even though her own name begins with <S>, Sarah usually represented /s/ in her writing with <C> because of the similarity between the beginning of the letter name <C> and the sound /s/ (note her spelling *tickets* as *TAKc*). She uses <V> for the /th/ in thank and the and to represent /f/ in for. Noteworthy also is the <I> in Suns. Sarah consistently used <I> to represent the schwa, as she did here. (Particularly interesting

Figure 4-4. Sarah's thank-you note for basketball tickets.

about Sarah's art for this thank-you note is that in the picture she drew of the Suns basketball team she included two baskets, five players, and one basketball.)

When /r/ is salient as in a blend or a schwa *r*, (<or>, <er>, or <ir>), Sarah pronounced /r/ and wrote it with <r> (for example, she would spell *teacher* as *tehr* and *roar* as YR, as seen in the cover illustration).

A third sound influenced by Sarah's perception and pronunciation was /h/. This one was particularly difficult for her, probably because she did not hear the sound of its letter name and it is the only sound articulated in this way. The <h> at the end of her own name is part of the schwa and was no help to her in clarifying what letter to use to represent this sound. Sarah invented two solutions for this pattern in her writing. In the solution she used most consistently, <Y> represented /h/. As mentioned earlier, the beginning of the letter name <Y> sounds like /w/ which is why she represented /w/ with <Y>. Since /h/ and /w/ both involve an aspiration, this may also explain her representing /h/ with <Y>.

Sarah usually referred to the <Y> symbol for /h/ by it's letter name (*why*) but not always. Once, in writing to our friend Terri, Sarah, four years ten months, spelled *house* as *YAYS*. I asked her to name the letters in *house* to clarify that spelling for me. She referred to the <Y>s as "foo foo," adding "It says *hu*," making a /h/ sound as in house. (She pronounced *house* as *hows*. The first <Y> represented /h/ and the second <Y> represented /w/.) Because she knew this was not her usual use of <Y> she invented another name, *foo foo*, for the symbol.

Sarah's other solution to /h/ appeared in a get-well card to a friend in her class, Jonny, when he had his tonsils removed (see Figure 4-5). After Sarah, four years ten months, read me her letter to Jonny, I pointed to the unfamiliar curvy symbol near the end of the first line and asked her to tell me about it. I said I knew the other letter names like <d>, <l>, <N>, and <e>, but I was not sure of that one. She replied, "That's foo foo. It says *hu*," making the /h/ sound as in *hope*. Perhaps she was consciously creating a symbol for her earlier *foo foo* written as <Y>, perhaps not. In either case she was not sure what to do with /h/ and invented a new symbol and name until she gained more experience and learned how to represent that phoneme in English. This was the only time this invented symbol appeared, probably because Sarah realized it was not a symbol she saw in her environment. It was another placeholder that allowed her to continue writing and share with Jonny her concern for him.

In the get-well card Sarah begins Jonny's name with <d> because of the articulatory similarity between /dĵ/ and /d/. In both sounds the tip of the tongue is positioned at the upper gums. She spells *Dear* as *dA*, without representing /r/, but does use <R> in *BATR* to represent the schwa *r*. She again represents /s/ in *miss* with <C> and /f/ in *feel* with <V>. It was about this time that Sarah began writing her name in all uppercase letters. While /h/ was difficult for Sarah, she did use <h> to represent the <ch> letter combination as in *teacher*, which she spelled *tehr*.

Sarah's basic rule was to spell according to her perception and

dA dI Ne I   e
Dear Jon-ny, I ho-
                    (hope)

P   U   VeL BATR
pe you feel better.

I MAC U
I miss you.

SARAH. I L   U
Sarah.   I love you.

Figure 4-5. Sarah's get-well card for Jonny.

phonology. Using that rule she made logical decisions as a writer and grew to be highly consistent in following her own invented system as she gained experience. Anyone looking at her writing without understanding her system would conclude that Sarah was simply writing arbitrary letters, that she didn't understand phonics yet, that she obviously didn't know letter-sound relationships and needed lots of help. Yet she had invented and perfected an incredibly sophisticated writing system and understood far more about phonics, phonology, and articulation than I did. Initially, whenever a new spelling pattern appeared in her writing, I fell into my old way of thinking and assumed she was guessing and writing randomly.

I quickly learned to trust her, though, to assume there was a reason, and to look for the explanation. There was nothing random or arbitrary about anything she did.

Phonics wasn't controlled or imposed on Sarah from the outside as an isolated program or method in any formal way; she invented it, made sense of it, and used it because she needed it and saw its function and purpose in her own reading and writing. She continually refined her phonics system and learned to control phonic relationships as she gained experience in making sense in her reading and writing. Sarah exemplified what Ken Goodman (1993) describes:

> Phonics is always both personal and social, because we must build relationships between our own personal speech (our idiolect), the speech of our community (our dialect), and the social conventions of writing. It is always contextual because the values of both sound and letter patterns change in the phonological, grammatical, and meaning contexts they occur in [as it did for Sarah in /r/ and /h/]. And it's never more than part of the process of reading and writing. For these reasons, phonics is learned best *in the course of* learning to read and write, *not as a prerequisite*. (51)

Sarah's art, when drawing was the clear dominant focus rather than writing (although these creations often included some writing), continued to develop during this time as she expanded her subject matter to include such things as houses with people in them, airplanes, animals, snowmen, angels, our church with the pastor at the altar, flowers, curved sidewalks, even the Statue of Liberty (I have no idea where that came from but she drew it a number of times). Her figures became more detailed, including necks, bodies, arms, and legs with dimensions rather than lines, and so on. She also individualized many of her drawings. If she was drawing her family, for example, she included glasses on her father since he wears glasses, and curly hair on me. When art was her focus, she worked to embed new details to express her meaning more precisely.

When Sarah's dominant focus was writing, however, her portraits and art became noticeably less integral to her work. The human figures were less detailed and without bodies; sometimes she included little or no art at all. Anne Dyson (1989) reports that whereas children's written texts sometimes begin almost as afterthoughts to accompany their drawings, gradually the texts take on and carry more meaning:

> [Children's] texts themselves will assume some of the functional power of their pictures and their talk, conveying their images and linking them to each other socially. Their texts will become more dynamic worlds that mediate between their own lives, those of their friends, and their experiences in the wider world. It is this process by which writing, through the children's activity, finds a niche in their artistic, social, and intellectual worlds. (14)

Drawing's original function of representing meaning became less adequate and essential for Sarah as she became more experienced with representing her meaning in written text and focused on understanding the intricate workings and relationships in our written language system.

Using Graphic Information to Spell   As Ken Goodman (1993, p. 71) has stated, "how the words sound" is only one way children try to make sense of written language. They also "remember what written words look like," including letters, letter combinations, shape, length, configuration, and so on. Visual information is something all literate persons use. Many of us have experienced writing a word and asking someone how that word is spelled because our spelling "doesn't look right" to us, according to our memory of the graphic form of the word. Simply by looking at a text we can tell whether or not it is written in English because of our knowledge of English spelling patterns and forms. Even if we are unsure of the language, we recognize letter patterns that are not English.

Young children also key into graphic forms and spelling patterns in their writing. Before they have had the experience with written language to understand the alphabetic principle, children write by drawing on orthographic information they perceive in their environment. The shape, form, and direction of their writing looks like the print they see, indicating their attention to graphic symbols in their sociocultural community (Harste et al. 1984).

Other research substantiates the influence of graphic information. Ferreiro and Teberosky (1982) found that children use two principles in deciding whether something is readable: one is quantitative—that the word have two to four, generally three, letters—and the other qualitative—that there is an internal variation in those letters. Both of these principles relate to the orthographic information in their environment.

Sarah's use of graphic information is evident. We saw a few examples of it in her spelling of her friends' names in Figure 4-3. She included some letters because she remembered seeing them, not because she heard and represented them.

Another example is Sarah's spelling of *kite* when she was four years ten months old. Originally she spelled *KIT* but erased the <K> and replaced it with <C>. In English /k/ is represented by both <k> and <c>, usually depending on the following vowel sound. As we saw in earlier examples Sarah fairly consistently used <K> to represent /k/ and <C> to represent /s/. *KIT* was a phonic spelling for her. When I asked her why she changed the <K> to <C> she replied, "Because *Casey* starts with <C>." Casey was one of Sarah's friends, and Sarah remembered that Casey spelled her name with <C> to represent /k/. Even though that contradicted the rule she had invented for her writing, she chose here to abandon her own phonics rule and use the graphic information from *Casey* to spell *kite* as *CIT*.

One of the most frequently used letters in English is <e>. It is not uncommon to find children incorporating <e> in their writing, even when they do not hear it as a phoneme. We saw an example of this in Sarah's spelling of *Alex* as *ALXSe* and in her spelling of *hope* in Figure 4-5. Whether she specifically knew *hope* conventionally includes <e> or not, she knew it is a common letter and incorporated it into her spelling.

A second example of Sarah, four years three months, using <e> as a graphic marker is in her birthday invitation list in Figure 4-6.

The <e> at the end of *Allison*, spelled *AISe*, again reflects Sarah's awareness that <e> is a common final marker found on English words as well as adds some length to a long name. While *Amber*, *Allison*, and *AJ* all begin with <A>, the initial phoneme in each is different. Sarah nevertheless represents the initial phoneme in each of these names with <A>, drawing on graphic information she sees and remembers. We also see graphic influences in her spelling of *Jessica*, *Phyllis*, and *Allison*, where she represents /s/ with <S> rather than <C>. (She also represents the /f/ in *Phyllis* and *fish* with <v> and writes <h> for /ch/ and <I> to represent the schwa in *teacher*.)

In her eagerness to be more like those she perceives as more experienced literate persons in her world, Sarah invented her own form of cursive

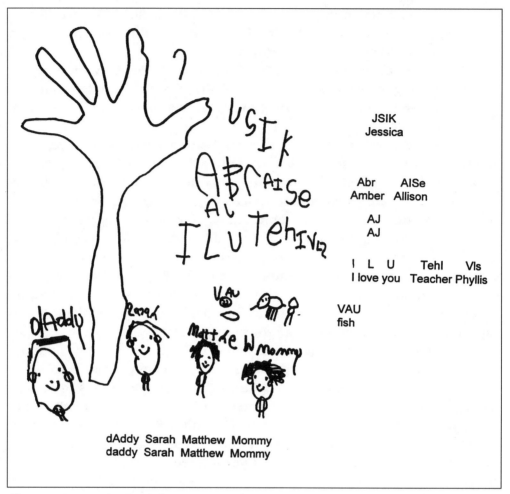

Figure 4-6. Sarah's birthday invitation list.

writing by connecting her letters, as she had seen adults connect theirs. An example of this is a thank-you note Sarah wrote to Terri for the gift Terri gave her on her fifth birthday (see Figure 4-7).

Sarah's cursive caused her to lose track at times of where she was and what she had written. When we were discussing her letter after she finished it, I questioned her about what looked like an <R> in *thank*. She explained that it was a "cursive k," picking up on a graphic feature of a lowercase cursive <k> resembling an <R>. Not to confuse her cursive <k> with her

I L U.
I love you.

SARAH.
Sarah.

dAY E Vak A Vo VI dAc.
Dear Terri Thank you for the dress.

VAK u FR V JIBOP.
Thank you for the jumprope.

Figure 4-7. Sarah writes <F> for the first time.

<R> in *SARAH* and *FR* (the second *for*) she distinguished her "cursive k" by forming it with a smooth stroke without a "loop" in the middle.

As Sarah's experiences with written language increased, she refined her perceptions of sounds and how she represented her perceptions graphically. An example of this appears in Figure 4-7. We've seen in earlier examples that Sarah regularly represented the phoneme /f/ with <v>. In writing this thank-you note (she insisted on beginning with her signature so Terri would know immediately who was sending it), she said her text under her breath as she usually did. When she finished, she looked at the paper and in an astonished voice announced, "I made an <F>!" She realized immediately (while I had to examine all of her previous writing samples to verify it) that in the last line of the letter she for the first time represented /f/ with <F>. It wasn't consistent yet (in the previous line she still represented the /f/ in the earlier *for* with <v>), but she was refining her perceptions and pronunciation to distinguish between the voiceless /f/ and the voiced /v/, which she reflected graphically in her writing. She again used <v> in thank and the, adding <I> to represent the schwa in the, another refining mark, although unconventional.

Sometimes we overlook or ignore the importance and role of graphic information in discussing writing, placing the sole emphasis on phonics. Remembering graphic patterns and sequences and how words look read plays a key role in children's learning how to spell.

Disequilibrium: The Mismatch of Systems   A childhood landmark is learning to write one's name. Names are important, for through them we identify who we are, what belongs to us, and those to whom we are speaking. Sarah became interested in and learned to write her name when she entered preschool at age three and a half. School often provides this intrigue and impetus for children (Taylor & Dorsey-Gaines 1988).

For the next fifteen months after learning her name Sarah wrote S-a-r-a-h everywhere, on school papers, letters, pictures, cards, in the church attendance book, everywhere. S-a-r-a-h was her name, her autograph. And it was the one piece of writing, along with the names of those in her family, that she had not invented how to spell, but just learned and accepted. It was her logo, her iconic representation of herself, a "picture" so to speak that she "drew" without understanding the orthographic and phonological relationships involved. She reproduced her name without question as a logographic whole (Lieberman 1985) . . . until March 3, 1993. On that day, when I came home from the university, Sarah presented me with a picture she had stenciled accompanied by her writing (see Figure 4-8).

I asked Sarah to read for me what she had written. She pointed and read, "Mommy. From /s ae wə/, [pronouncing *CAYI* by sounding and elongating the phonemes], SARAH." (Remember that she represented /s/ with <C>, that she pronounced /r/ as /w/, which she represented with <Y>, and that she used <I> to represent the schwa.) Sarah had invented how to spell her name, revealing that she was experiencing a real and personal disequilibrium, a reality all readers and writers eventually face: the orthographic and

Mommy VAM CAYI SA
Mommy From Sarah Sa-
(Sarah)

RAH.
rah.

Figure 4-8. Sarah invents how to spell her name.

phonological systems of our language do not match. She realized that there is a discrepancy between the graphics she sees and writes in S-A-R-A-H and the phonic rule system she was inventing. Perhaps she was wondering:

- Why does my name begin with <S> when <C> represents /s/ for me?
- How can there be two <A>s that *look* the same but have different sounds?
- Why is there an <R> where I hear /w/ that should be <Y>?
- Why are there five letters in my name when I only hear four sounds?

67

In addition, she was still considering the complex role of <H>, which she was not yet using in a conventional way. (In her name the letter combination <ah> represents a single schwa sound.)

There was nothing systematic or logical to her about the logographic S-A-R-A-H, based on the rules she was inventing. Again things "fell apart" for Sarah, but rather than being paralyzed, this time she confidently invented to make meaning. At the same time, she also recognized the stability of S-A-R-A-H, that it represented her to others in her world, so she included it. It had been a little more than two years since Sarah first distinguished between drawing and writing. Here she revisited that distinction, differentiating between drawing her signature iconically and writing it in her alphabetic system.

Sarah did not write *CAYI* every time she wrote her name, but over the next several weeks she included it, usually with *SARAH*, a number of times. Five weeks later she invented her name again on an Easter card to our neighbor. This time she spelled it *ZAYRI*, incorporating some of the graphic information from *SARAH*. She wrote five letters, added the <R> she saw but didn't pronounce, retained the <Y> for the /w/ she did pronounce, and used <Z> for the /s/ phoneme, possibly because they are closely related and <Z> looked more like the backwards <S> she usually wrote when she signed her name.

Over the next few months Sarah also invented spellings for the other names she had been writing as a single unit without inventing. She spelled *Mommy* as *MIME*, *Daddy* as *dAdE*, and *Matthew* as *MAVU*, using <V> to represent the /th/ and <U> to represent the /yu/. Up to two years later Sarah occasionally invented these and other spellings she knew conventionally, such as zoo, which she invented as *zuu*.

Sarah taught herself, as well as me, about phonics. She invented her own system for relating her phonology to print and constructed a personal understanding of phonics (K. Goodman 1993) she could never be "taught." As she gained experience with written language and presented and tested her invented system against the written language in children's literature, other print around her, and especially the spelling and phonics in her own name, she understood that there is more to spelling than a one-to-one relationship between letters and sounds. We have alternate spelling patterns for the same sound patterns and alternate sound patterns for the same spelling patterns. Spelling involves learning to integrate both graphic and phonological cues. That is a critical point all readers and writers eventually come to understand.

Sarah helped me see, through her invented spelling system, that perception, articulation, and pronunciation are not standard, yet spelling is. All phonics alone can do is provide a logical comprehensible spelling for a particular speller; it cannot be counted on to provide a conventional spelling since standard spelling is arbitrary, the result of human social decisions (K. Goodman 1993). For adults, phonics is relatively easy and straightforward and makes sense. Sarah helped me to consider complexities I took for granted and to appreciate children's accomplishment in learning to read, write, and spell.

Their name seems to be a logical place for some children to confront and come to terms with this issue in a powerful and unavoidable way, as Sarah did. No matter what other or how much writing children do, nothing is as personal, significant, and constant for them as writing their name.

Punctuation

Punctuation is the means by which authors share with readers necessary information about meaning or language structure not contained in the words of a written text. Punctuation is unique to written language. Oral language is a continuous stream of sound we hear in a span of time. We usually have no difficulty making sense of the complex syntax of oral language because we have the benefit of sounds, grammatical patterns, volume, vocal speed, facial expressions, situational context, intonation, pitch, stress, and juncture to guide us (Martens & Goodman 1996). We hear the excitement in a speaker's voice, observe his or her gestures and expressions, and attend to the situational context of the conversation for cues to facilitate making meaning.

We are more constrained in expressing feelings, emotions, and intonation in writing. Written language is constrained to flat two-dimensional space and can use only punctuation to clarify the text. The sentence structure in written language needs to be simpler than that in oral language or our writing would be incomprehensible (K. Goodman 1993). Written language is constrained by syntactic rules and grammatical divisions and by marks signifying meaning to support, clarify, and enhance written messages for the reader (Martens & Goodman 1996).

When I was teaching, I believed that children learned about punctuation and how and when to use it through controlled direct instruction and practice. Sarah taught me otherwise. As she invented purposes for writing, such as notes, signs, letters, stories, or lists, and forms to frame those functions, she also invented how to punctuate. As she perceived punctuation, specifically periods, in the written language around her and how others in her community used punctuation, she understood the need for punctuation to clarify her writing for her readers. She invented hypotheses for when and how punctuation functions and incorporated punctuation into her own writing to both represent meaning and segment written language into units.

Punctuation to Represent Meaning   Fonts and graphics are not usually considered punctuation, but they are nevertheless a means through which authors represent and communicate personal feelings and written meanings. Sarah invented ways to use fonts and graphics to enrich and punctuate her meanings. She placed a heart in her letter to Jonny (see Figure 4-5) to express her love and concern and on valentines to send her love to her family and friends. She used the size of her *YR* (*Roar*) to indicate volume and emphasize the ferociousness of her dinosaur (see cover illustration). She invented and used her own font of "puffy letters" as well as incorporated color in particular ways at particular times. Her handprint (see Figures 3-6-B and 4-6) became a way she embedded herself and her personhood into her work in order to declare her self-awareness, individuality, industriousness, and ownership (Fein 1993).

Punctuation to Segment Written Language   Spacing and punctuation marks are two ways to segment written language to convey meaning and make it more comprehensible to the reader. Some children first begin segmenting their written language by spacing their words. Sarah didn't incorporate spacing into her writing until she was well into kindergarten.

Instead of spacing Sarah began segmenting her written language with periods. She became aware of them and their function of marking "the end" or "stop," as she said, through her reading and through hearing Matthew talk about them. Sarah first punctuated with periods in her "songwriter" (see Figure 3-4-A) to indicate to the singer it was time to stop singing. Her periods disappeared after that, perhaps because she was concentrating on understanding other aspects of written language. When she felt more comfortable with that understanding, she revisited the concept of using periods.

We have already seen examples of Sarah's punctuating with periods in Figures 4-5, 4-7, and 4-8. Figure 4-9, a thank-you note Sarah, five, wrote to her grandparents for a birthday gift, is another example.

Sarah began this note *Dear . . .* , not *I love you*. When she finished writing *boc* (*book*), she said "That's the end" and placed the period after *boc*. She then wrote her name followed by the period, and finally the *ILU* and period at the top of the paper. As she was setting the paper aside she glanced at it and said, "Oh wait," took the paper back, and placed a period after the <E> in the fourth line, which is at the end of a line but not at the end of her spelling of *Pinocchio*. After staring at it with a perplexed look for several seconds, she said, "Oh, that's not the end," crossed out her period, and then set the paper aside.

Sarah's system for when and when not to insert periods was deliberate, and systematic. While not fully conventional, she used her periods to mark the end of segments of her text: an *I love you* greeting, the letter itself, and her name. She monitored herself and never placed a period in the middle of a word. As she continued to gain experience with written language, she refined her hypothesis and punctuated between sentences and also used other forms of punctuation, such as commas, question marks, and exclamation points.

Sarah's spellings also continue to be systematic here, based on how she perceives and pronounces phonemes. She represents /g/ in *Grandpa* and *Grandma* with <K> because of the articulating similarity in /g/ and /K/. The times she represents /k/ in this letter, as in *VAC* (*Thank*), *PNOCEO* (*Pinocchio*), and *BOC* (*book*), she uses <C>, rather than her usual <K> for that phoneme, perhaps because she already used <K> for /g/. Here she spells *the* as *LI*. The <L> reflects the articulatory similarity between /l/ and /th/ and indicates a refinement in her perception from her original spelling of *the* as *v* to represent /f/. With both /l/ and /th/ the tip of the tongue is positioned at the upper front teeth whereas with /v/ the upper front teeth are positioned at the lower lip. The <I> represents the schwa she hears. What again look like arbitrary letters continue to be systematic and logical within her invented system.

Sarah invented additional uses for periods, in keeping with her hypothesis

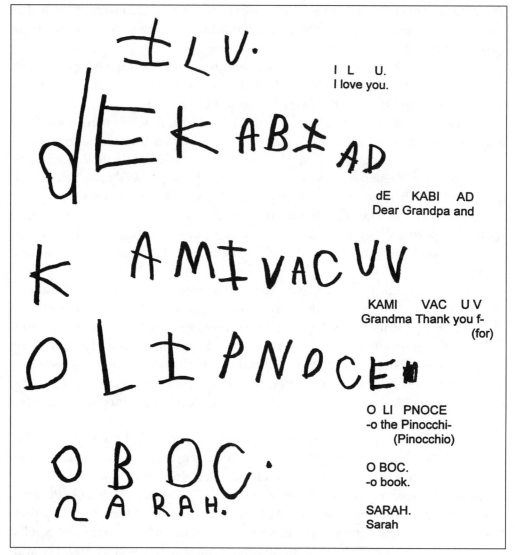

Figure 4–9. Sarah uses periods in a thank-you note.

of marking segments of text with them. Just as she placed a period to indicate the end of her own name, she began indicating the end of other names also, particularly in her birthday lists. When she listed her friends to invite to her birthday party, she began marking the end of each name with a period.

While this is not a conventional use of periods, with it Sarah demonstrated her awareness that periods mark the end of linguistic units and that she was grappling with the concept of "sentenceness."

Reading Like a Writer, Writing Like a Reader

The hours Sarah spent transacting with children's literature, reading by herself and listening as others read to her, profoundly influenced her literacy. She helped me understand more deeply how reading and writing support each other and thus how important it is for children to have time and opportunities to experience, explore, and invent in both areas simultaneously. Immersed in the beauty, power, and richness of literature, she, as a writer herself, mined the literature for insights to help her refine her own literacy, particularly in her use of graphic and phonological information in her own writing.

Learning Graphic and Phonological Information Through Literature

In her experiences with literature Sarah gathered graphic and phonological information that enabled her to refine her perceptions and her writing inventions. One example of this is in her use of the numerals *2* and *4* as rebuses or logographs for the words *to* and *for*, respectively. The only time Sarah intermixed letters and numerals in her writing was in this instance. We saw an example of this earlier in Figure 4-2.

Sarah's invention of representing *to* with *2* and *for* with *4* was not supported as she transacted with literature, though. The only times *2* and *4* are used in text is to represent numbers. So, after about nine months of gaining more experience with written language, she abandoned that invention and began writing *to* as *tu* and *for* as *vo*. One of the first instances of this was in the thank-you note for basketball tickets in Figure 4-4. As her experiences with reading, writing, and literature continued to grow she refined those spellings to their standard forms.

Reading literature also influenced and strengthened Sarah's perception and understanding of the relationship between the orthography and phonology of English. We discussed earlier Sarah's difficulty with /h/ and how to represent it in her writing. *Spot's Birthday Party* (Hill 1982) was a familiar and favorite book Sarah often selected to read. During one particular reading when she was four years ten months old, she was following the text with her finger. On one page she pointed and read, "How did you find me?" As she was turning the page, she casually commented, "<H> says *hu* like *How*." When I asked her how she knew that, she turned the page back, pointed to the <H> in *How* and said, "Because *huh*." Other less obvious examples that Sarah was reading like a writer include the letter patterns she used in her writing reflecting English and her more conventional representations of phonemes and meaning. Time and experience with literature and other forms of print in a variety of settings are critical to children's literacy.

> [Young readers] use their memory of how words look as a check on their inventions—which is why it's important that they both read *and* write as they learn written language. Because they check their invented spellings against the spellings they find in their reading, the authentic texts found in real children's books are the real basis of their growing awareness of spelling conventions. (K. Goodman 1993, 71)

The perplexities Sarah encountered as she wrote, she researched as she read, checking her invented solutions and hypotheses against other written texts. Literature helped her refine her perceptions and inventions.

Learning How to Write Through Literature

Reading and transacting with children's literature also influenced Sarah's composition of stories. As children read stories and listen to stories being read to them, they develop a sense of story that becomes the foundation from which they write their own stories. The books they read serve as models for their growing knowledge of the content and conventions of written language (Terry 1989). They write the kinds of texts they read. If they are immersed in rich, authentic literary texts, they write more complex sentences and a wider range of forms than children exposed only to basal-type texts (DeFord 1981).

As a reader and a writer, Sarah examined the texts she read and used them as models in her writing. She read like a writer to gain the knowledge of a writer and to learn how to write like a writer. All competent writers, no matter how young, use authors in this way (Smith 1991). Sarah's first "stories" were all *I love/like* personal narratives, drawing on the knowledge, feelings, and experiences she knew best—her own. As she became more experienced with life, language, and literature, however, her stories became more imaginative and she drew on her experiences with literature as well as her personal interests and experiences for content. One of her stories, for example, involved Snow White and Beauty and the Beast. Another, which she wrote in church during the sermon one Sunday morning, featured Captain Hook. In the story Sarah drew on her knowledge of Captain Hook from *Peter Pan* to write her personal ending. The *Peter Pan* video, a favorite of hers at the time, ends with Hook swimming away, the crocodile hot on his heels. In her story Sarah decided that Captain Hook was eaten by the "shark." She drew no picture to accompany her story, embedding her meaning only in the written text.

Stories were not the focus of Sarah's writing at this point. Since we read her wonderful stories every day, writing stories perhaps wasn't as functional and authentic to her as other writing. She did write some stories, however, including books on particular topics such as Christmas. As Frank Smith (1982) states, "The development of composition in writing cannot reside in writing alone, but requires reading and being read to. Only from the written language of others can children observe and understand convention and idea together" (p. 195).

Integrating the Graphophonic System into Reading

As Sarah became more aware of print she tried to weave the graphophonic system with the semantic-pragmatic and syntactic systems of language. Her reading made sense and sounded like language; now she wanted to connect her reading with the print.

Sarah had several self-initiated strategies for integrating print and reading. Writing played an important role. Through her writing she confronted the "essential problem—how meaning is conveyed through, and retrieved from, the print" (Dyson 1984, p. 168). She read like a writer and wrote like a reader, inventing how the systems relate and refining her inventions. Another strategy Sarah used was finding familiar "landmarks," such as *I*, *no*, *Mommy*, or *yes*, as she read, pacing her reading so her finger and voice reached the landmarks at the same time and rereading to perfect the timing if they didn't.

Even without specific landmarks Sarah used her knowledge, experience, and familiarity with text to follow the print. If there was text "left over" she would go back and reread. For example, one day when she was four years ten months, she was reading *Spot's Birthday Party* (Hill 1982). One portion of the text read "Don't forget me!" As Sarah read she pointed only to *Don't* but read the entire sentence. Then, noticing that there was text remaining, she went back and reread, pointing and reading, to connect the oral meaning she knew and said with the written text she saw.

As Sarah's awareness of visual cues increased and she integrated the visual information in the text with the nonvisual information in her head, her reading slowed down considerably. Slowly and carefully she read and reread clauses and sentences, predicting meaning, using print to confirm her predictions, and correcting herself if it didn't.

Learning to integrate the graphophonic system so that it works in concert with the syntactic and semantic-pragmatic systems requires time, patience, and practice. As Sarah began to follow the print intensely, she occasionally overrelied on it and did not produce a response that sounded like language (syntactic system) and had meaning (semantic-pragmatic system). An example occurred when she, age five, was reading *Good Night, Jesse!* (Ziefert & Smith 1990). In the story Jesse stalls so she does not have to go to bed. On one page the text is lined in this format:

"I can't, Mom.
My drawer is open."

Just as Sarah turned to this page, she glanced down and said, "Look, there's *Mommy*! Only part of it is down here" (pointing to the *My* beginning the second line). She combined *Mom* from the end of the first line with *My* from the beginning of the second line to produce *Mommy*. If Sarah had read *Mommy* for *Mom* she would not have disrupted the meaning of the text. But combining *Mom* and *My* as she did indicated she was overrelying on graphophonic cues at the expense of syntactic and semantic-pragmatic cues, as well as orthographic cues such as the period after *Mom* and the uppercase <M> in *My*.

An overreliance on graphophonic cues is not uncommon when children are learning how to integrate those cues with the syntactic and seman-tic-pragmatic systems. I learned not to correct Sarah immediately and thus focus her on "getting the words right." I began to understand the impor-tance of Sarah's learning to control her own reading without continual inter-ruptions from me. We discussed that reading must always make sense (Does that make sense?) and sound like language (Does that sound like language?), and that she needed to monitor her reading for sense and sound. As she be-came more experienced, reading a wide variety of genres in a wide variety of contexts for a wide variety of purposes, Sarah fine-tuned her reading inven-tion for herself, strengthening and deepening her understanding that read-ing is a process of sampling, inferring, predicting, and self-correcting, if necessary, always with a focus on constructing meaning by integrating the graphophonic, semantic-pragmatic, and syntactic cues together. Sarah learned to be an independent responsible reader, who takes risks, monitors, and solves problems for herself. She taught me the importance of support-ing her while at the same time allowing her to assume responsibility for her reading.

Expanding and Refining Literacy

Like all readers and writers, Sarah continued to refine her literacy, expand-ing her understanding of what we "do" with written language and inventing how she can read and write. She was consciously aware, though, that for her inventions to be understood by others she needed to situate them within the boundaries of the societal agreements that allow us to share meaning ef-ficiently and effectively with each other.

The more Sarah wove reading and writing into her everyday life, the more reasons she found to read and write. She discovered "the range of functions served by written language, including its capacities for social inter-action and individual reflection" (Dyson 1989, p. 12). The "range of func-tions" produced genres for Sarah. Without hesitation she invented not only reading and writing but the forms, particularly of writing, to fill functions and purposes she needed. As she had distinguished between drawing and writing, she fine-tuned her distinction between the functions and purposes of written language. "Genres" became her new theme (Rowe 1987), and it is here that Sarah's writing expanded quickly and here that her inquiries "What are *you* doing with that written language?" "How can *I* read and write?" "How do *we* read and write?" converged more precisely as she sought to reflect, participate, and interact with others and have her inventions be understood by members of her community.

In addition to the thank you letters, songwriting, art, birthday invitation lists, greeting cards, "I love/like" personal narratives, stories, and maps, she also invented birthday signs, notices for her bedroom door, matching games, board games, book lists, math homework, dot-to-dot games, and job charts.

Sarah entered kindergarten as a sophisticated reader and writer in need of opportunities to continue to test and refine her inventions for functional authentic purposes in a literacy-rich environment and community. Would she find those opportunities?

5

Sarah in Kindergarten

On August 23, 1993, five-year-old Sarah radiated excitement about her first day of kindergarten. She was awake, dressed, and ready to leave for school, her backpack brimming with new school supplies, long before it was time to head out to the car to go. Her expectations about all the fascinating things she would learn, the tantalizing books she would hear and read, the imaginative stories she would write, the challenging math problems she would solve, and the numerous new friends she would make couldn't have been higher.

Sarah entered kindergarten that day not as a neophyte to literacy but as an experienced reader and writer who was knowledgeable about written language and confident about herself and her ability to invent and solve problems she confronted in making sense in her reading and writing. She entered kindergarten seeking rich, functional, meaningful experiences with literacy to broaden, deepen, and extend her understanding and support her as she continued to refine and sharpen her reading and writing and grow as a citizen in our society.

Unfortunately, those aren't the kinds of experiences she encountered in school. The literacy she experienced at school contrasted sharply with the literacy she knew and experienced at home. At home she still continued to invent reading and writing for authentic purposes. For example, about the time school started, Sarah wrote a letter to an adult friend, Sue. Sue's mother had just died and Sarah wanted to express her sympathy and love (see Figure 5-1). On the first day of kindergarten, however, Sarah brought home a worksheet she had completed that tested her fine motor control. On it, she had traced the dotted zig-zag path to help one frog find another.

Growing in her desire to write stories at home, she wrote about a fox

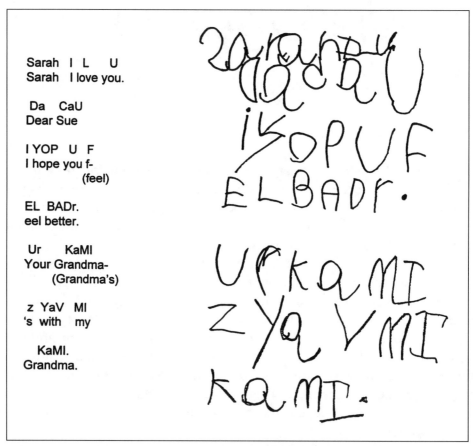

Sarah I L   U
Sarah I love you.

Da   CaU
Dear Sue

I YOP U F
I hope you f-
          (feel)

EL BADr.
eel better.

Ur   KaMI
Your Grandma-
      (Grandma's)

z YaV MI
's with   my

  KaMI.
Grandma.

Figure 5-1. Sarah's letter written at home to Sue; Sarah referred to Sue's mother as *grandmother* because Sarah's grandmother had died a few months earlier.

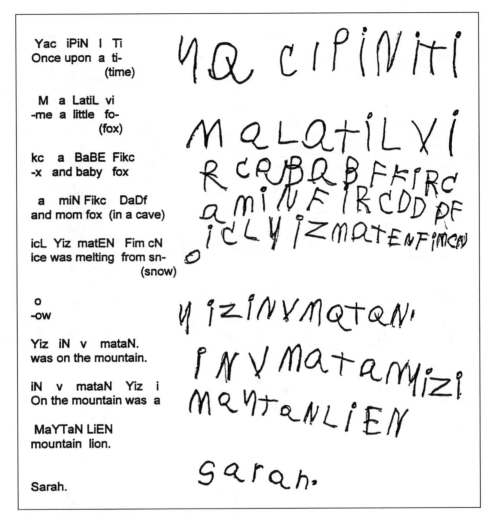

Yac iPiN I Ti
Once upon a ti-
(time)

M a LatiL vi
-me a little fo-
(fox)

kc a BaBE Fikc
-x and baby fox

a miN Fikc DaDf
and mom fox (in a cave)

icL Yiz matEN Fim cN
ice was melting from sn-
(snow)

o
-ow

Yiz iN v mataN.
was on the mountain.

iN v mataN Yiz i
On the mountain was a

MaYTaN LiEN
mountain lion.

Sarah.

Figure 5-2. Sarah's story written at home.

family and a mountain lion on a snowy mountain (see Figure 5-2). At school, she worked on her handwriting, moving through the alphabet one letter at a time, practicing forming her letters correctly and staying within the lines (see Figure 5–3).

Sarah was more and more intrigued with math and mathematical concepts, which showed up in her writing at home. She experimented and invented aspects such as how to write addition notation (see Figure 5-4). At

Figure 5-3. Sarah's handwriting sheet done at school.

school, math consisted of a worksheet with four groups of objects. In each group, Sarah was to circle the two objects used in the same way.

Sarah's most treasured friend and companion was a toy stuffed dalmatian dog, Lucky, one of the 101 Dalmatians. Lucky went everywhere with Sarah, including school, but one day he was taken from the play area next to the school where Sarah left him to sit during recess to watch her play. At home Sarah, extremely upset and distressed, made a poster, which we copied to pass out to every classroom in the school, asking if anyone had found Lucky (see Figure 5-5). At school she worked on phonics, completing a worksheet on which she marked the two pictures in each row that began with the same sound.

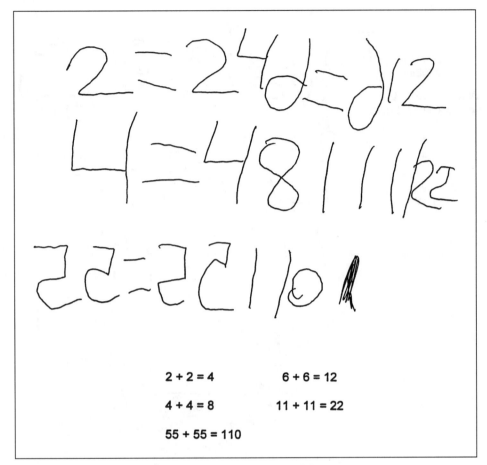

2 + 2 = 4   6 + 6 = 12

4 + 4 = 8   11 + 11 = 22

55 + 55 = 110

Figure 5-4. Sarah's invention of how to write addition.

There are many other similar examples contrasting Sarah's literacy at home and her literacy at school. The teacher did have the children write in journals several times a week, but usually on assigned topics. The children were also asked to respond to literature the teacher read to them, but they did so on worksheets that constrained their thinking and interpretation of the story.

And so the year progressed. Sarah and her classmates sat at their desks in school doing worksheets and restrictive assignments to ensure they had the necessary visual and motor skills so they would become ready to read and write. At home, Sarah, and I'm confident her classmates as well, were

3230849.
3230849

Wav u CEN LikE.
Have you seen Lucky?

Sarah.
Sarah.

i Liv LikE.
I love Lucky.

i Lik LikE.
I like Lucky.

Figure 5-5.   Sarah's poster for Lucky created at home; what look like *R*s in Lucky are Sarah's cursive *K*s.

reading and writing to meet authentic, meaningful, personal, and social needs and purposes. Sarah's enthusiasm for school dwindled. Her experiences with literacy were not considered or honored; her knowledge about literacy was not respected or built upon; her reading and writing inventions were not valued or welcome. Her literacy was censored and she was disenfranchised.

My fears had come true: Sarah had a teacher like I was, one who didn't value who the children were as literate human beings, who didn't provide opportunities for them to teach her what they knew about literacy, who didn't celebrate their literacy inventions. Sarah and her classmates were forced to "accept a stereotype of language that is contrary to the insights [they] gained from [their] own experience" (Halliday 1973, p. 3), just as my students had. A sharp dichotomy existed between literacy at home and literacy at school. At home literacy was "meaningful, contextualized, and in the broadest sense social" (Halliday 1973, p. 12), a complex cultural activity intrinsic and relevant to life; at school it was meaningless and decontextualized, taught as an abstract skill with no consideration for what reading and writing are for in the lives and futures of the students (Szwed 1988).

There was also a sharp dichotomy between how Sarah and her classmates were viewed as literate persons and how they no doubt viewed and continued to construct their views of themselves as literate. At home they were competent, intelligent, responsible members of the literate community who were accepted and treated as card-carrying members of the literacy club (Smith 1988). They initiated and participated in natural everyday literacy events with literate others who understood the importance of newer members "learning on the job," because as their experiences broadened and deepened, so would their knowledge and understanding. In school Sarah and her classmates were inexperienced children, with little background, knowledge, and understanding about reading and writing. Their learning and activities were controlled and corrected. They were handed bits and pieces of information about a motor skill through drills and work bearing little resemblance to the literacy they experienced in their world.

Sarah's teacher, (like I was years ago), was by no means intentionally indifferent or disinterested, nor was she uncaring toward her students. She, like me, was a concerned, loving teacher intending to provide her students with what she believed was the solid foundation necessary for literacy. But she, like me, was operating from a set of beliefs about learning, literacy, and children that dictated, controlled, and constrained what she saw and how she taught.

If I could turn back the clock or if I enter a kindergarten classroom again in the future, what would I do differently? What did I learn from Sarah that would impact my classroom and my relationship and experiences with my students? What do I want Sarah's and Matthew's teachers to believe and understand about children, learning, and literacy?

6

Lessons from Sarah

Sarah is a master teacher. Her classroom is the world in which she and I, her student, live. She teaches by providing captivating demonstrations that intrigue and pique my curiosity, challenging my beliefs and inviting me to pose and investigate my own inquiries. As with all great teachers, she is a learner too, always using what she knows to learn what she doesn't know, always taking risks to expand her understanding and push herself to higher expectations, always refining her literacy and deepening her knowledge, and always collaborating with those around her to enrich her own and others' learning.

The lessons Sarah taught, and continues to teach, cut to the core of my beliefs and are forever changing the way I view children, learning, and literacy. She taught me to always be a kidwatcher (Y. Goodman 1985); she made me aware of the multiple ways we make meaning and impressed on me the importance of encouraging other learners to explore them; and she made the learning process visible and enabled me to understand it from a new and informed perspective.

Kidwatching

Kidwatching is "learning about children by watching how they learn" (Y. Goodman 1985, 9). Kidwatchers daily observe children reading, writing, speaking, and listening in different settings. They look for evidence of language development, and reflect on what the child's responses tell them about the child's knowledge of language (Y. Goodman 1978). Children's unexpected reading or writing responses, in particular, open a window into their thinking, hypotheses, and ways of organizing the world. These responses are not mistakes or errors but evidence of their learning and growth. Through conversations and observations, kidwatchers crawl into the mind of a child and take on the child's perspective of learning and literacy.

Sarah taught me the significance of using her as my informant to teach me what I don't know about her and about literacy, which always propels my own insights and learning. She taught me not to assume, not to unquestioningly impose my beliefs and views of the world as an interpretation of her acts. She taught me the importance of always asking questions and the consequences of not asking them.

One particular incident made the importance of asking questions indelibly clear. One evening when I arrived home, I found on the table a paper Sarah, three years seven months, had colored at preschool. She had colored only a portion of one of the figures in the picture, and there was a sticker in the upper left-hand corner of that side of the paper. When I turned the paper over, I found a series of symbols written in a circular format. Sarah's name was on this side, written by the teacher in the upper right-hand corner upside down from what appeared to be the upright orientation of Sarah's writing. (Sarah *did* know how to write her own name at this time).

I called Sarah from her bedroom and asked her about what she'd written on the back side of the paper. She replied, "I wrote the ABCs." Since I didn't know she could even *say* the ABCs much less write them (we had done neither in any formal sequential way at home), I was intrigued and curious and said, "Show me." I watched as she began toward the upper left, pointing to her symbols, left-to-right, around the paper, reciting a letter of the alphabet as she pointed to each symbol. When she had written her alphabet, she had curved her writing whenever she came to the edge of the paper and continued moving around in the next possible direction, producing a "circular" alphabet in the process. When she was unsure of how to produce a letter, she had inserted a placeholder. The only letter she did not write was <N>. As she pointed and recited, she ran <M> and <N> together making them sound as one, as often happens when singing or saying the alphabet. She knew and had already written and referred to <N> in other contexts, though. She wrote <B> for <P> and <U> for <Q> because their names sound and are pronounced similarly. (Sarah wrote this alphabet during the period of time when she was reluctant to write, realizing there was a lot she didn't know about the written language system. It was a week *after* this that she wouldn't write at all for several weeks, until she discovered her "stick" placeholder while writing "Thank you for the money.")

The next day I visited Sarah's preschool teacher to understand the context in which Sarah had written her alphabet. The teacher was quite surprised and had no idea that Sarah was writing the alphabet. She had not inquired about Sarah's writing when she went around putting names on the papers while children worked and had not inquired about her writing when she put stickers on the papers at the conclusion of the activity. Had I not asked Sarah either, this literacy event and the knowledge it evidenced would have gone completely unnoticed.

By observing and questioning the students and reflecting on what they know and see, kidwatchers get to know learners, their knowledge, their questions, their strengths, their strategies, and how they think, thereby gaining insights into how to support them in their learning. In seeing language, learning, and the world through the eyes and mind of the child, kidwatchers learn how to offer the right response at the right time to propel the learner. That's how I knew to provide Sarah with a strategy that liberates for the future, like her "stick," rather than a direct correct answer that satisfies for the moment. Strategies, I learned, create independent, resourceful, confident learners and problem solvers rather than ones who don't trust themselves and their abilities and are dependent on others for answers and solutions. Seeing through the child's mind and eyes also reveals the child's hypotheses and thinking. It's because I examined Sarah's literacy artifacts as a kidwatcher that I discovered her sophisticated reasonings in creating her invented phonics and writing system.

Kidwatching is an exciting experience that takes kidwatchers to places they never imagined existed. I know—Sarah's taken me there. She taught me to be a kidwatcher, that in being a kidwatcher I am always a learner too.

Multiple Ways of Making Meaning

Our world is saturated with authentic, meaningful, functional events and experiences in which we make and share meaning with others through a variety of sign systems. These sign systems include oral language, written language, art, music, math, gesture, play, dance, movement, and so on. My original focus as a teacher and parent studying Sarah's literacy was only on language. I was so concerned with immersing Sarah in a rich print environment and with how that environment influenced, supported, and enhanced her language learning that I never considered the many other ways of making meaning that we naturally weave into our lives. I never considered how these multiple ways of coming to know were influencing the ways in which Sarah was sharing her meaning.

Sarah opened my eyes to language's not being the only or necessarily the most efficient way to communicate meaning. Making meaning involves more than language. Daily, in addition to reading the newspaper or writing notes and lists, we also listen to music, balance the checkbook, count silverware with which to set the table, sing, doodle while we think, discuss or evaluate logos or paintings, count the minutes or hours someone is late. We count while we play piano, draw or sketch while we talk on the phone, and measure with spoons and cups while we read a recipe. Logos combine art and writing, musical jingles accompany text on the TV screen, gas station signs provide the price of gasoline, dancing or rhythmic movement accompanies music and songs, . . . the list goes on and on.

Children are not just immersed in a print-rich environment, they are immersed in an environment rich with multiple ways through which we communicate meaning. Just as children are not oblivious to the print, they are not oblivious to these other ways of sharing meaning. It is logical, then, that children will not just invent reading and writing, but seamlessly weave those inventions with inventions in other sign systems to share meaning.

Written language, my original foremost concern, was not the original primary sign system Sarah used to share meaning. Her reading and writing appeared "couched within other symbolic media" (Dyson 1989, 7) through which she was already communicating, including play, gesture, song, oral language, and art. Communicating in these multiple ways made her aware that she could represent meaning symbolically, a necessary understanding critical to being a reader and writer. Art played a particularly vital role in her writing, which I have tried to highlight. It was her experiences with and control of her drawing and her <o>s that was the catalyst and scaffold, liberating and propelling her to create and represent meaning through written language.

As I watched Sarah flow effortlessly between art, music, math, play, and language, I became aware of how she selected the system (or systems) through which she could best communicate the meaning she wanted to share and invented how to shape her meaning into that form, working within the natural constraints of that system. To write in English, for example, she was constrained to letters and words written left to right and from the top to bottom of the page. She thought like an artist to draw; she thought like a mathematician to use numbers; she thought like a cartographer to draw maps; she thought like a musician to create her songwriting and so on. She took a particular perspective on her meaning and invented how to make meaning in that particular system. In so doing she expanded and pushed the boundaries of her meaning potential and enhanced her general overarching ability to create and share meaning.

Sarah made me reflect back on all the times in kindergarten that I got impatient with my students because they took so long drawing in their journals that they ran out of time for the "important business" of writing. I thought about how I focused and constrained my students by channeling them into writing and never allowed them to continue exploring how to think in other sign systems and invent how to communicate meaning in these systems. It never occurred to me, for example, that even though I exposed the children to music, I could also have set up a center and provided opportunities and time for them to explore and invent music as well as how to write it. I wonder how much my own, and other's, insecurity and lack of confidence in themselves to draw, paint, do math, or sing may be related to our not being encouraged and supported in exploring and inventing how to think and share meaning in these other systems when we were young.

Sarah made me face how naive and verbocentric I had been in believing language was *the* way to communicate. While language is certainly a common and central way we share meaning in our society, and critical to know, if it was our only communication system, sharing meaning would be boring and less efficient and our world would be stripped of its beauty and richness.

The Learning Process

I taught kindergarten as though literacy was a commodity the students acquired by proceeding through a sequenced series of steps or stages, each of which contained isolated bits of information to be mastered, such as letters and sounds, punctuation, and spelling, each of which built on the previous one, during the school year and from year to year, and each of which stood alone, without the support of other ways we create, share, and enhance meaning. Accuracy and convention, achieved through drills and practice ordered, controlled, and orchestrated by me, were the hallmarks of "real" reading and writing. Sarah shattered those beliefs. Supported by my reading, thinking, and talking to others, I saw through Sarah how using language naturally, in an authentic, meaningful context, makes learning easy, that my sequenced hierarchical model of how learning occurs was an erroneous representation of the reality of learning.

Keeping Language Whole

Sarah helped me crystalize what I had been reading: language is indeed its own teacher (Y. Goodman & Altwerger 1980). In natural everyday use, language is complex, but children relish that complexity. When language is whole and used in context, children have multiple cues from which to draw in understanding how language works. They sort out patterns and rules and invent how to make sense of and with it, as Sarah did. That's how they learn to speak and that's how they learn written language most easily.

The language systems I deemphasized as a teacher in the primary classroom, namely the semantic-pragmatic and syntactic systems, were Sarah's, strengths. Those two systems were what she initially controlled best and built on to understand and make sense of reading and writing. She focused on integrating the graphophonic system with the other two when she saw the reason and necessity for it to refine her reading and writing. She integrated it in her way, in her time because of her experiences with language, when she was ready.

When language is kept whole and children have the voice and power to use it for relevant, authentic purposes meaningful to them, language learning is easy (K. Goodman 1986). Complexity comes for children when we step in and try to make learning "easier" by breaking it up into bite-sized pieces. We don't speak, read, write, or listen one letter, sound, or skill at a time and neither do we learn that way. We learn to orchestrate all the parts of language in meaningful harmony by controlling and using them in concert for our own authentic purposes.

The Learning Cycle

As I observed, questioned, and talked to Sarah, I came to see that literacy learning was not the neat and orderly sequenced and controlled process I had believed it to be. Quite contrary to being linear, the process as Sarah helped me see it is cyclical, allowing for zigs and zags, revisiting, and rethinking. It is a process propelled by the inquiries learners pose based on the perception and understanding that grow out of their experiences. Driving and influencing the process for each particular learner are the sociocultural community, time spent in personal and social experiences with literacy in a variety of different contexts, and inquiries.

Sociocultural Community   Learning does not occur, and learners do not live, in a vacuum. Learners are part of a social community in a sociocultural environment. The understanding Sarah constructed and the personal inventions she created were influenced and constrained by the sociocultural community in which she was an active member, accepted and respected as an observer and participant in literacy events. As she sorted through and made sense of reading and writing for herself, she moved from observation to interaction and transaction.

Personal and Social Experiences with Literacy   Every learner has a unique personal and social literacy history shaped by his or her personal and social literacy experiences (Y. Goodman 1990, 1992). Complex literacy configurations, including how and why literacy is used personally and socially in everyday life, vary from individual to individual in numerous ways: the amount of time spent reading and writing; the number, variety, and richness of literacy opportunities available and taken advantage of; the variety of contexts for reading and writing, such as home, community, school, church, and so on; and the responses, attitudes, and values toward literacy of others in one's environment.

For Sarah, the time, opportunities, experiences, and contexts were rich and unending. Those factors, not her intelligence, were the primary influences on her inventions and her learning. No other child's experiences, responses, or inventions will be identical to Sarah's for no other child's personal and social histories are identical. While the social and personal literacy histories of each child differs, all children do have their histories and experiences and strengths on which to build. The homes and communities in our society, including inner-city areas (Moll et al. 1992; Taylor & Dorsey-Gaines 1988), are saturated with print. Families and individuals use reading and writing for many different purposes particular to them, which may or may not provide literacy experiences schools value and expect (Taylor 1982). The challenge for us as teachers is to discover those experiences, regardless of their variety and complexity, and build on them by providing numerous functional purposes for reading and writing in the classroom.

Perceptions Learners' perceptions of their literacy experiences generate and propel their curiosity. Perhaps their perceptions are based on their interests, perhaps on a question or disequilibrium, or perhaps on some salient feature of print or in an event that has captured their attention. When experiences are limited, perceptions are more broad and global; with more experience perceptions become more detailed and precise.

When Sarah was a young toddler, with limited experience with literacy, her perceptions focused on understanding the whole of written language, what it was and how it made sense, and on how she could convey meaning through her wavy lines of print. As she became more experienced her perceptions zeroed in on finer aspects of written language, how the parts relate to and make sense within the whole and how she could control those parts in the context of the whole. The more experience she gained the finer her perceptions and the more detailed her inventions of how language works. Beginning with the details of language would have been nonsense to her: without an understanding of the whole the details are meaningless.

Our perceptions as adults work in a similar way. With little background and experience, we first have broad, global perceptions, which gradually become more precise. If we are learning to knit, for example, we focus first on holding the needles and manipulating them with the yarn to make basic stitches. The more experienced we become the more we fine-tune our perceptions and abilities based on what we need to know and how the parts work within the whole, using our growing background information on which to ground new understanding, new perceptions. In knitting, as we gain experience we tackle more involved stitches and patterns.

Generating Inquiries and Inventing Solutions   As we perceive, we ideate (K. Goodman et al. 1987), or think about what we've perceived. From the perceptions we don't understand or that are anomalies we generate our inquiries. Our inquiries, not necessarily conscious, are puzzlements that tickle our curiosity. Neither do our inquiries occur one at a time; we research multiple inquiries simultaneously as Sarah did with "What are *you* doing with that written language?" "How can *I* read and write?" "How do *we* read and write?"

We respond to our inquiries by drawing on our background knowledge and experiences, researching, and inventing a solution. We present our inventions in our community, reflect on the responses we receive from others (either their acceptance and comprehension or lack of it), revise our inventions, and invent again, over and over. Gradually as we gain experience and our knowledge deepens and broadens, we refine our inventions.

Refining Inventions   We've seen how Sarah refined her inventions, gradually moving them within the boundaries of written language that allow us to share meaning with each other. Her revisions and refinements were continual. She didn't form "bad habits" and continue to use the "wrong" inventions when I didn't correct her, as I used to worry my students would do if I didn't correct them. She knew her inventions were temporary and freely revised them when they no longer worked or she had new information to integrate into them. Some inventions, like her <v> to represent the letter combination <th>, she used for quite a while until she gained the experience to refine her perception. She also, I suspect, used that and some other inventions as temporary placeholders while she perceived and focused on other aspects of written language; she couldn't deal with every intricate detail at once. I think her "themes," such as her *I love/like* personal sentence starter or her lists, also functioned as a placeholder in this way, allowing her to focus on an aspect of written language as she used the theme over and over.

The point to be emphasized and celebrated is that Sarah was not afraid to try to read, write, and spell when she knew she wasn't "right." She took risks and freely tested and refined her inventions. Because of that, at *no* point was her learning ever at a standstill. The few times "correctness" was her concern, her learning was very limited.

The more experience Sarah gained with language in a variety of rich contexts, the finer the aspects of written language she perceived, which called for more precise inventions and revisions of those inventions. Sarah showed me that learning isn't always moving from topic to topic in a forward direction, though. It entails circling back and revisiting an earlier understanding with new information and refining that understanding with new insight. Sarah revisited her initial separation of drawing and writing, for example, when her <o>s became placeholders (see Figure 3-3) and again with her name when she realized the orthographic and phonological systems of English are not a simple one-to-one match (see Figure 4-8). She also showed me that learning includes having things "fall apart" when new insights don't fit with present understanding. Things "fell apart" for Sarah when she realized the relationship between written and spoken language through her *ILU* and when she invented how to spell her name (see Figure 4-8). Both occurrences prompted her to rethink, reorganize, and refine her understanding. Experiences of revisiting and having things "fall apart" were not regressions for Sarah nor are they regressions for any child; rather, they mark a refinement and enrichment of understanding.

As Sarah refined her inventions and they appeared more "conventional" it was not because she was "adding" new knowledge or information to her understanding; everything she needed to know was always present before her in the whole of the context, supporting her. The more she refined her inventions, the clearer and more meaningful those details and conventions became. She continually used what she learned to refine and invent again, outgrowing herself and her understanding and expanding her potential to make meaning. As Piaget (1970) said, "Each time one prematurely teaches a child something he [sic] could have discovered for himself [sic], that child is kept from inventing it and consequently from understanding it completely" (715).

And so the cycle continues. New inquiries grow from old or generate on their own. We invent other ways to communicate meaning, as Sarah did in math, art, and music, and we use multiple systems of meaning to support and enhance our understanding and perspectives. Learners are empowered when they are trusted to be responsible and in control of their learning, when they are respected and valued as literacy colleagues in the literacy club.

Inquiry in Education   Inquiry such as Sarah's has proven to be a powerful framework for education (Short & Harste with Burke 1996), one that creates and propels lifelong learners. In inquiry-driven classrooms students are provided time and opportunities to invent, play, and experiment with written language and other sign systems in a variety of contexts for a variety of authentic purposes. Teachers and students negotiate curriculum. Teachers understand that learning happens in rich literate communities where learners' knowledge and experiences with literacy and the world are celebrated and expanded on. Students' interests and experiences outside school are welcomed in the classroom; there are no artificial barriers between literacy at home and literacy at school. Students have time to think, reflect, and explore their personal wondering as well as collaborate with others, using multiple sign systems for meaningful purposes.

Lifelong Learning   Sarah made me see and understand that literacy learning is a multifaceted, multidimensional process that continues throughout our lifetime. She taught me that there isn't one moment or step in a learning sequence at which learners can suddenly read and write. She showed me that what distinguishes the reading and writing of adults from the reading and writing of young children is not a difference in the literacy process but a difference in their control of the process. My years of experience with literacy, for example, have provided me with infinitely more occasions than Sarah has had to "practice" reading and writing for a variety of authentic purposes in a myriad of meaningful contexts, all of which have made me a more proficient reader and writer. Sarah hasn't yet experienced the luxury of those years of reading and writing that afford her the time, information, and opportunities she needs to gain greater control of the literacy process (Y. Goodman 1992; Harste et al. 1984). Her literacy may not appear as "traditional" or "conventional" as mine, but she taught me that that does not infringe on or devalue its authenticity, legitimacy, importance, or value.

Literacy learning never ends for any of us; we never know all there is to know to make us totally proficient on all topics in all genres. We never completely and fully "arrive." There will always be more to discover and learn as we encounter opportunities to read and write in new contexts, in new genres, for new purposes.

An Invitation

As my teacher and collaborator in learning, Sarah inspired me to generate my own inquiries into understanding literacy and the learning process, what they are and how they relate to each other. Just as Sarah did, I invented ideas and hypotheses, revised, revisited, and had things "fall apart"; pushing the boundaries of my own beliefs was not easy or painless. Sarah forced me to examine and evaluate my conventional notions of literacy that created an exclusive literacy club open to accurate readers and correct spellers and tear down the barriers to create an inclusive literacy club open to and made up of lifelong learners. While literacy conventions are important and necessary, Sarah made me see they are not and should not be used as gatekeepers.

My hope in writing this book is that as Sarah taught me to see differently, she will help others see differently, too, with a deeper appreciation for children, literacy, and the learning process. No discussion recapping and describing being her student can compare to or represent the richness of learning directly from and with her. I invite you, though, to examine your own beliefs; to evaluate your own definition of literacy and who it includes and excludes; to reflect on your teaching and classroom practices to see that they respect the literate lives, knowledge, and multiple ways your students are inventing to communicate meaning; and to be a kidwatcher, looking for how your students can teach you what they know as your literacy and curricular informants (Short & Harste with Burke 1996). I invite and challenge you to "see" what you know with enriched perception, enlightened eyes, and informed understanding.

Professional References

Baghban, M. 1984. *Our Daughter Learns to Read and Write: A Case Study From Birth to Three*. Newark, DE: International Reading Association.

Bissex, G. 1980. *Gnys at Work: A Child Learns to Write and Read.* Cambridge, MA: Harvard University Press.

———. 1984. "The Child as Teacher." In *Awakening to Literacy*, ed. H. Goelman, A. Oberg, and F. Smith, 87–101. Portsmouth, NH: Heinemann.

Cohen, E. P., and R. S. Gainer. 1995. *Art: Another Language for Learning.* Portsmouth, NH: Heinemann.

DeFord, D. 1980. "Young Children and Their Writing." *Theory Into Practice* 19 (3): 157–162.

———. 1981. "Literacy: Reading, Writing, and Other Essentials." *Language Arts* 58 (6): 652–658.

Doake, D. 1985. "Reading-like Behavior: Its Role in Learning to Read." In *Observing the Language Learner*, ed. A. Jaggar and M. T. Smith-Burke, 82–98. Newark, DE and Urbana, IL: International Reading Association and National Council of Teachers of English.

———. 1988. *Reading Begins at Birth*. New York: Scholastic.

Duckworth, E. 1987. *The Having of Wonderful Ideas and Other Essays on Teaching and Learning.* New York: Teachers College Press.

Dyson, A. H. 1984. "Reading, Writing, and Language: Young Children Solving the Written Language Puzzle." In *Composing and Comprehending*, ed. J. Jensen,

165–175. Urbana, IL: ERIC Clearinghouse on Reading and Communication Skills and the National Conference on Research in English.

———. 1989. *Multiple Worlds of Child Writers: Friends Learning to Write*. New York: Teachers College Press.

Fein, S. 1993. *First Drawings: Genesis of Visual Thinking*. Pleasant Hill, CA: Exelrod Press.

Ferreiro, E. 1980. "The Relationship Between Oral and Written Language: The Child's Viewpoint." In *Oral and Written Language Development and Research: Impact on the Schools*, ed. Y. Goodman, M. Haussler, and D. Strickland, 47–56. Urbana, IL: National Council of Teachers of English.

———. 1984. "The Underlying Logic of Literacy Development." In *Awakening to Literacy*, ed. H. Goelman, A. Oberg, and F. Smith, 154–173. Portsmouth, NH: Heinemann.

———. 1990. "Literacy Development: Psychogenesis." In *How Children Construct Literacy: Piagetian Perspectives*, ed. Y. Goodman, 12–25. Newark, DE: International Reading Association.

———. 1991 "Literacy Acquisition and the Representation of Language." In *Early Literacy: A Constructivist Foundation for Whole Language*, ed. C. Kamii, M. Manning, and G. Manning, 31–55. Washington, DC: National Education Association.

Ferreiro, E., and A. Teberosky. 1982. *Literacy Before Schooling*. Portsmouth, NH: Heinemann.

Goodman, K. 1986. *What's Whole in Whole Language?* Portsmouth, NH: Heinemann.

———. 1993. *Phonics Phacts*. Portsmouth, NH: Heinemann.

———. 1994. "Reading, Writing and Written Texts: A Transactional Socio-psycholinguistic View." In *Theoretical Models and Processes of Reading*, ed. R. B. Ruddell, M. R. Ruddell, and H. Singer, 1093–1130. Newark, NJ: International Reading Association.

Goodman, K., E. B. Smith, R. Meredith, and Y. Goodman. 1987. *Language and Thinking in School: A Whole-Language Curriculum*. New York: Richard C. Owen.

Goodman, Y. 1978. "Kid Watching: An Alternative to Testing." *Journal of National Elementary Principals* 57 (4): 41–45.

———. 1980. "The Roots of Literacy." In *Claremont Reading Conference Forty-Fourth Yearbook*, ed. M. P. Douglass, 1–32. Claremont, CA: Claremont Reading Conference.

———. 1983. "Beginning Reading Development: Strategies and Principles." In *Developing Literacy: Young Children's Use of Language*, ed. R. P. Parker and F. A. Davis, 68–83. Newark, DE: International Reading Association.

———. 1984. "The Development of Initial Literacy." In *Awakening to Literacy*, ed. H. Goelman, A. Oberg, and F. Smith, 102–109. Portsmouth, NH: Heinemann.

———. 1985. "Kidwatching: Observing Children in the Classroom." In *Observing the Language Learner*, ed. A. Jaggar and M. T. Smith-Burke, 9–18. Newark, DE and Urbana, IL: International Reading Association and National Council of Teachers of English.

———. 1990. "Discovering Children's Inventions of Written Language." In *How Children Construct Literacy: Piagetian Perspectives*, ed. Y. Goodman, 1–11. Newark, DE: International Reading Association.

———. 1992. "Early Literacy Development: A Sociotransactional View." In *Selected Proceedings From the First Whole Language Umbrella Conference: Perspectives on Whole Language: Past, Present, Potential*, ed. M. Bixby, D. King, S. Ohanian, S. Crenshaw, and P. Jenkins, 16–22. Columbia, MO: University of Missouri-Columbia.

———. 1993. Personal Communication.

Goodman, Y., and B. Altwerger. 1980. "Reading—How Does It Begin?" In *Discovering Language With Children*, ed. G. S. Pinnell, 81–85. Urbana, IL: National Council of Teachers of English.

Hall, N. 1985. "When Do Children Learn to Read?" *Reading* 19 (2): 57–70.

———. 1987. *The Emergence of Literacy*. Portsmouth, NH: Heinemann.

Halliday, M. A. K. 1973. *Explorations in the Functions of Language*. New York: Elsevier.

———. 1980. "Three Aspects of Children's Language Development: Learning Language, Learning Through Language, Learning About Language." In *Oral and Written Language Development Research: Impact on the Schools*, ed. Y. Goodman, M. Haussler, and D. Strickland, 7–19. Urbana: National Council of Teachers of English.

Harste, J., V. Woodward, and C. Burke. 1984. *Language Stories and Literacy Lessons*. Portsmouth, NH: Heinemann.

Huck, C. 1990. "The Power of Children's Literature in the Classroom." In *Talking About Books: Creating Literate Communities*, ed. K. Short and K. M. Pierce, 2–15. Portsmouth, NH: Heinemann.

Lark-Horovitz, B., H. Lewis, and M. Luca. 1967. *Understanding Children's Art for Better Teaching*. Columbus, OH: Charles E. Merrill Books.

Leichter, H. 1984. "Families As Environments for Literacy." In *Awakening to Literacy*, ed. H. Goelman, A. Oberg, and F. Smith, 38–50. Portsmouth, NH: Heinemann.

Lieberman, E. 1985. *Name Writing and the Preschool Child*. Unpublished doctoral dissertation, University of Arizona, Tucson.

Martens, P. 1994. *"I Already Know How to Read!": Literacy Through the Eyes and Mind of a Child*. Unpublished doctoral dissertation, University of Arizona, Tucson.

Martens, P., and Y. Goodman. 1996. "Invented Punctuation." In *Learning About Punctuation*, ed. N. Hall and A. Robinson. Portsmouth, NH: Heinemann.

Matlin, M. 1984. *Transitions into Literacy: A Working Paper* (Occasional Paper No. 10). Tucson: University of Arizona, College of Education, Program in Language and Literacy.

Mikkelsen, N. 1985. "Sendak, *Snow White*, and the Child as Literary Critic. *Language Arts* 62 (4): 362–373.

Moll, L., C. Amanti, D. Neff, and N. Gonzalez. 1992. "Funds of Knowledge for Teaching: A Qualitative Approach to Connect Households and Classrooms." *Theory Into Practice* 31 (2): 132–141.

Piaget, J. 1970. "Piaget's Theory." In *Carmichael's Manual of Child Psychology*, ed. P. H. Mussen, 703–732. New York: John Wiley & Sons.

———. 1971. *Psychology and Epistemology.* New York: Grossman.

Platt, P. 1975. "The Three R's in Art: Reading, 'Riting, and Roleplaying." In *Focus: Elementary Art Education*, ed. A. Caucutt, 58–65, Reston, VA: National Art Education Association.

Read, C. 1971. "Pre-school Children's Knowledge of English Phonology." *Harvard Educational Review* 41 (1): 1–34.

Rosenblatt, L. 1978. *The Reader, the Text, the Poem: The Transactional Theory of the Literary Work.* Carbondale, IL: Southern Illinois University Press.

———. 1983. *Literature as Exploration.* New York: The Modern Language Association of America.

Rowe, D. 1987. "Literacy Learning as an Intertextual Process." In *Research in Literacy: Merging Perspectives*, Thirty- Sixth Yearbook of the National Reading Conference, ed. J. E. Readence and R. S. Baldwin, 101–112. Rochester, NY: National Reading Conference.

Schickedanz, J. A. 1990. *Adam's Righting Revolutions: One Child's Literacy Development From Infancy Through Grade One.* Portsmouth, NH: Heinemann.

Short, K., J. Harste, with C. Burke. 1996. *Creating Classrooms for Authors and Inquirers.* Portsmouth, NH: Heinemann.

Smith, F. 1976. "Learning to Read by Reading." *Language Arts* 53 (3): 297–299, 322.

————. 1982. *Writing and the Writer*. New York: Holt, Rinehart and Winston.

————. 1988. *Joining the Literacy Club*. Portsmouth, NH: Heinemann.

————. 1991. "Appendix: Reading Like a Writer." In *Interwoven Conversations*, ed. J. M. Newman, 362–374. Portsmouth, NH: Heinemann.

Szwed, J. F. 1988. "The Ethnography of Literacy." In *Perspectives on Literacy*, ed. E. R. Kintgen, B. M. Kroll, and M. Rose, 303–311. Carbondale, IL: Southern Illinois Press.

Taylor, D. 1982. "Translating Children's Everyday Uses of Print Into Classroom Practice." *Language Arts* 59 (6): 546–549.

————. 1983. *Family Literacy: Young Children Learning to Read and Write*. Portsmouth, NH: Heinemann.

Taylor, D., and C. Dorsey-Gaines. 1988. *Growing Up Literate: Learning From Inner-city Families*. Portsmouth, NH: Heinemann.

Terry, C. A. 1989. "Literature: A Foundation and Source for Learning to Write." In *Children's Literature in the Classroom: Weaving Charlotte's Web*, ed. J. Hickman and B. Cullinan, 49–60. Needham Heights, MA: Christopher Gordon.

Vygotsky, L. 1983. "The Prehistory of Written Language." In *The Psychology of Written Language*, ed. M. Martlew, 279–292. New York: John Wiley & Sons.

Wells, G. 1985. *Language, Learning and Education*. Philadelphia: NFER-NELSON.

Whitmore, K. 1992. *Reaching Potentials: The Personal and Social Language and Literacy Histories of 3–8 Year Olds* (Occasional Paper No. 22). Tucson: University of Arizona, College of Education, Program in Language and Literacy.

Whitmore, K., and Y. Goodman. 1995. "Transforming Curriculum in Language and Literacy." In *Reaching Potentials: Transforming Early Childhood Curriculum and Assessment*, Vol. 2, ed. S. Bredekamp and T. Rosegrant, 145–166. Washington, D.C.: National Association for the Education of Young Children.

Children's Literature References

Allard, H. 1981. *The Stupids Die*. New York: Trumpet.

Brown, M. W. 1947. *Goodnight Moon*. New York: Scholastic.

Carle, E. 1975. *The Mixed-up Chameleon*. New York: Scholastic.

DePaola, T. 1975. *Strega Nona*. New York: Scholastic.

Dijs, C. 1990. *Are You My Mommy?* New York: Simon & Schuster.

Fox, M. 1986. *Hattie and the Fox*. New York: Trumpet.

Herman, G. 1990. *Time for School, Little Dinosaur.* New York: Random House.

Hill, E. 1982. *Spot's Birthday Party*. New York: G. P. Putnam's Sons.

Hutchins, P. 1972. *Goodnight Owl!* New York: Macmillan.

Keats, E. J. 1962. *Snowy Day*. New York: Scholastic.

Martin, B. 1989. *Chicka Chicka Boom Boom*. New York: Scholastic.

———. 1990. "The Gingerbread Man." In *Sounds of Children at Play on the Hill*, ed. B. Martin Jr., P. Bergan, and J. Archambault. Allen, TX: DLM.

Moerbeek, K. 1988. *Who's Peeking at Me?* Los Angeles: Price Stern Sloan.

Sendak, M. 1963. *Where the Wild Things Are*. New York: Harper Trophy.

Stowell, G. 1976. *Bright and Beautiful.* Belleview, MI: Lion Publishing Corporation.

Williams, V. B. 1990. *More More More*. New York: Scholastic.

Wood, D., and A. Wood. 1984. *The Little Mouse, the Red Ripe Strawberry and the Big Hungry Bear*. Singapore: Child's Play.

Ziefert, H. 1990. *The Wheels of the Bus*. New York: Random House.

———. 1991. *Sometimes I Share*. New York: Harper Collins.

Ziefert, H., and M. Smith. 1990. *Good Night, Jessie!* New York: Harper & Row.

Credits

Excerpts from "Piaget's Theory" in *Carmichael's Manual of Child Psychology*, edited by P. H. Mussen. Copyright © 1970. Reprinted by permission of John Wiley & Sons, Inc.

Excerpts from *GNYS at Work: A Child Learns to Write and Read* by G. Bissex. Copyright © 1980 by the President and Fellows of Harvard College. Reprinted by permission of Harvard University Press.

Excerpts from Dyson, *Multiple Worlds of Child Writers: Friends Learning to Write* (New York: Teachers College Press, © 1989 by Teachers College, Columbia University. All rights reserved.), pp. 7, 12, 14. Reprinted by permission of the publisher.

Excerpts from "Three Aspects of Children's Language Development: Learning Language, Learning Through Language, Learning About Language" by M. A. K. Halliday. In *Oral and Written Language Development Research: Impact on Schools*, edited by Y. Goodman, M. Haussler and D. Strickland. Copyright © 1980. Published by National Council of Teachers of English. Reprinted by permission of the publisher.

Excerpts from *Hattie and the Fox* by Mem Fox. Copyright © 1986 Mem Fox. Reprinted with the permission of Simon & Schuster Books for Young Readers.

Excerpt from "Kidwatching: Observing Children in the Classroom" by Yetta Goodman. In *Observing the Language Learner*, edited by Angela Jaggar and M. Trika Smith-Burke. copyright © 1985 by the International Reading Association. All rights reserved. Reprinted by permission of the publisher.

Excerpt from *The Reader, The Text, The Poem: The Transactional Theory of the Literacy Work* by Louise M. Rosenblatt. Copyright © 1978 by Southern Illinois University Press. Reprinted by permission of the publisher.